CHANGING TIMES:

RAMBLINGS OF AN OLD FART

– CHANGING TIMES –
RAMBLINGS
of an Old Fart

ESSAYS

by

MARSHA GORDON

Cover art by Doug MacGregor

Marsha Gordon
P.O. Box 51424
Fort Myers, FL 33994
transompublishing@gmail.com

Large Print Edition

ISBN #0615870244
ISBN-13 #978-0615870243

ACKNOWLEDGMENTS

No one writes a book in a vacuum. It takes many people to put the words on a page. Karen Auriti edited and formatted my ramblings. She was there at every comma and semi-colon, every character quirk and everything else involved in putting a book together. I began referring to it as "our book." Karen, thank you so much.

Brian Auriti's technical wizardry brought the book up to snuff for the publishing arena.

Doug MacGregor, cartoonist, illustrator and author, created the old fart on the cover. She certainly is an eye-catcher.

This collection of essays started as an exercise in a writing class and took on a life of its own. William Dietzel, Ph.D., and the members of his class encouraged me. Many thanks.

My daughter, Sari, was the first to read each desperate draft. She is a kind critic, but not *too* kind. I also thank Rick, Sari's husband, for the endless reams of paper and his computer support.

The creative souls in WeWrite, my critique group, reviewed each essay with literary acumen and made each line better. Thanks to each of them for their fellowship.

I'm beginning to feel like an Oscar winner without her notes. Thanks to all the others. You know who you are.

Marsha Gordon

TABLE OF CONTENTS

Changing Times

The times, they are a-changin'. (Bob Dylan)

Changing Places

We may not remember where we've been, we may not know where we are, but we are always somewhere.

Changing Parts
Changing parts will not make a Rolls Royce out of a Ford.

Changing Seasons
Deep in December, it's hard to remember...
(with apologies to The Fantasticks)

Changing Loyalties
Country and family are two sorts of loyalty.
We don't need any more.

Changing Diapers
Babies change our lives in so many ways.

Changing Minds

Mankind's gentle dreams, how quickly they turn into nightmares! (Donald Duck)

Changing Clothes

Beware of all enterprises that require new clothes. (Henry David Thoreau)

Changing Tires

Be sure your spare is properly inflated – a life lesson.

Changing Views

If you never change your mind, why have one? (Edward deBono)

Changing Tides

The tides are constant. We have no control.

Changing Times

The times, they are a-changin'.
(Bob Dylan)

1

ALLIGATOR ALLEY AND PHISH

It was December 30, 1999, two days before the Millennium. I was on my way to Fort Lauderdale to complete an interview for The National Institutes of Health. My assignment: to interview senior citizens about their sex habits. *Why? To see what I'm missing?* I should be done by 3:00, back on the Alley by 4:00 and home just after dark.

Ahead was a rest stop. There were eleven tie-dyed Volkswagen vans in the parking lot. Eleven! Even in the '50s, I never heard of eleven of those painted buses together. I pulled into the rest stop to see what was going on.

Coming toward me was a group of aging, longhaired hippies, looking to be in their late 40s, early 50s. They were wearing jeans with holes and patches. Their tie-dyed shirts were bright with creative stars or concentric circles. They looked as though they'd know about those buses.

"Hey, wha's happenin'", I asked. *Darn, is that hippie talk or rap?*

Whatever it was, a tall man, his hair neatly pulled back in a long grey braid, wearing patched jeans and a star shirt, answered me. "What do you want to know, Little Mama?"

"What are you all doing here and what's the story behind all those vans?" I asked.

3

"Goin' to the Phish concert tomorrow night. Gotta be a day early for that. Our vans? All our vans are kept up for long trips, all the time. Nobody wants to miss a Phish concert."

"Oh, okay. Thanks."

What in the world is a fish concert? And why would you need to get there a day early? I had no idea.

I got to Fort Lauderdale, finished the sex interview with a 60-year-old woman and realized what I was missing... *every day*.

The timetable was perfect. I was back on the Alley at four. But I didn't get home until after dawn the next morning.

The day was clear. There was little traffic. I set my cruise control and enjoyed the ride, looking for gators and wildflowers.

One of the painted vans came up behind me but didn't pass. Soon there was a procession of vans following me. I supposed they were on their way to the Phish concert.

I'd been on the road for about an hour when I spotted a problem ahead. Traffic was stopped, but there were no brake lights. It looked as though they'd been there quite a while.

There were VW buses, passenger cars, big semis and pick-up trucks. I got out of my car and walked up the line a bit. Perhaps I could find the reason for this blockade. I was surprised to see that many of the passenger cars and pickups carried Phish fans.

Music was everywhere. Walking toward me was the man I had talked with at the rest stop.

"Well, greetings, Little Mama. We're gonna be jammed up here for at least a coupla hours. Happens every Phish concert. You have water, snacks? Probably not. Let's walk back to your car."

We did and he took me to the van right behind me. He spoke to the driver. "This here's Little Mama. I don't think she knows anything about Phish. Probably thinks it's a grouper show. We met back at the rest stop. She needs water, food and maybe a bathroom. Can you help her out, Darren?"

"You betcha, Wayne. Come on by later for a drink. I've got plenty." My new best friend nodded his head and left.

Darren got two bottles of water and a sandwich and walked me to my car. He was very serious when he said, "Now listen, Little Mama, I have to trust you. If you're hungry or thirsty or scared, or have some questions or just want company, come over to my van. My wife would really like to talk with you. She can tell you about bathrooms. Okay? Here's something to eat and drink for now."

"Thanks. I do have questions. What's Phish? Who are you all? The license plates are from all over the country." I stopped to take a breath and Darren jumped right in. Here's a recap of his answers:

Phish is an American rock band that got together at the University of Vermont in 1983. They're an eclectic band that plays, according to Wikipedia, rock, jazz, progressive rock, psychedelic rock, hard rock, funk, folk, bluegrass, reggae, country, blues, avant garde, barbershop quartet and classical music. Phish was the first band to permit fans to record concerts, and now to videotape them. They rarely get radio play and remain known mostly to those who discovered them while in college. They have a mighty fan belt – maybe it's all those vans.

Phish fans are mostly professional people or are well employed. Some have trust funds, like my friend Wayne. No wonder they can afford to keep those old vans so well maintained.

I ate my sandwich, drank my water and went for another walk. What a magnificent night; no humidity, no bugs, temperature in the low 70s and a full moon over the Everglades, bright enough to illuminate the River of Grass. I saw "civilians" who chose to stay in their cars and roll up their windows as Phish folk walked by. I felt sorry for them.

Wayne got out of his van when he saw me and introduced me to so many people, all of whom offered me food, drink, precious tape recordings and pot.

I went back to Darren's van and met his wife, Kate. It was time to learn about bathrooms. There are a couple of ways to accomplish necessary bodily functions. Most of the vans had a potty and I was welcome to use theirs. Or, every fifteen or twenty vans, long, narrow ditches had been dug. I could straddle one of those and a group of people, their backs to me, would stand in front of me, a human privacy screen. I opted for straddling, despite the warning about snakes.

Kate offered me soap and water, tea and cookies. I accepted them all and we chatted away like a couple of friends in a tea parlor.

I thanked her and went back to my car for a nap. I could sense people checking on me during the night. The windows were open and a cool, dry breeze blew through the car.

I awoke to a cacophony of horns blowing and motors revving up. The sun was rising. Wayne came by with a much needed donut and a precious Phish tape. Darren came by with coffee. What a great neighborhood. He pulled me out of the car and put his finger to his lips. I could hear, "Good Morning, Little Mama," spread from vehicle to vehicle.

I hugged my new friends and cried a little.

It had been an astonishing night during which I had been the "different" one. I had dared to step out of my comfort zone and been greeted with caring and respect. The feeling was mutual.

Historical Note: The concert was held in the Big Cypress Indian Reservation in the Florida Everglades. There were major New Year's Eve concerts around the globe including Sting, Barbra Streisand, and Billy Joel. Phish had the largest attendance of any concert that evening with 85,000 attendees, and every one of them was on Alligator Alley.

IT'S TIME

What's the hurry? It seems we're always trying to catch up, get to work, get home. Grab something quick for dinner and rush to be on time for bowling, gin rummy, mahjong. Rush to take the sitter to her house. Finally, home. A quick shower to save time in the morning. Then to bed until the alarm clock rings, interrupting the best dream of the night.

Rushing through life is nothing new. In 250 BC, the Greeks built the first alarm clock. A water clock told time by how fast the water went down. Eventually the water hit a mechanical bird and a loud screeching birdcall sounded throughout the compound, waking everyone. In 1787 the first mechanical alarm clock was created. It went off only at four in the morning.

Man used the sun, moon, planets and stars to measure the passage of time. Man also divided time into minutes with sixty seconds, hours with sixty minutes, days with twenty-four hours, weeks with seven days and so on.

In 3500 BC, the obelisk, a tall slender piece of wood, began measuring the days. It measured the longest day and shortest day. But it didn't work at night or on cloudy days. The sundial was the next time tracker in 1500 BC, but it had the same limitations.

The first wristwatch was created in the early 1600s when a gentleman tied a piece of string around his wrist and hung his pocket watch on it. Not long ago I bought a digital watch. Doesn't work for me. It just doesn't convey a sense of urgency like hands on a clock face.

What is this need to know the time of day, or how long a chore or a game lasts? In the 2012 Olympics, a race was won (and lost) by 9/10 of a second.

What is this obsession? Are we more competitive? Do we have such a strong urge to be first? Do we have too much to do to complete what is before us?

We are creating new time measurements: Nano and pico seconds are but two of them. A nanosecond (ns) is one billionth of a *second*. One ns is to one second as one second is to 31.7 years. A picosecond (ps) is one trillionth of a second. A ps is to one second as one second is to 31,700 years. We use these measures mostly in electronics. Even faster measures have been developed.

"Excuse me, someone is calling. I'll be back in a nanosecond. I won't even try for a picosecond."

THE CLOCK IS IN THE OVEN

My daughter, Sari, has become accustomed to the strange questions and requests I have been asking of her lately.

The other day, I called her to ask if she had a younger brother. I thought his name was Billy. She patiently explained that I had three children and that she was the youngest. There were none after her. Maybe Billy was a vivid dream.

Yesterday I asked Sari to take the clock out of the oven. "Okay, Mom." There was no hint of judgment, sarcasm or fear in her voice.

Aha! This time there was a good reason for my odd request. As I was getting ready for bed the night before, a low-battery beeping began. I have three remotes next to my bed. I took each one, separately, into the kitchen. The beeping continued from my bedroom. I could not think of any other battery-operated remotes.

Then I remembered. It was not a remote. The new battery clock was beeping.

I certainly couldn't sleep with all that noise. I tried to think of the most soundproof place in the house. It had to be the oven.

I put the clock in the oven and had a good night's sleep.

So there!

BUILT-IN OBSOLESCENCE

Warning: Products manufactured today
may have a predetermined life span

My computer stopped working last week. Not a warning, not a gasp, not a sigh; it just died. I punched all the keys I could think of. Not even a flutter. I called my son-in-law, who knows about these things. Rick tried everything he knew but couldn't bring it back.

"What about my files, Rick?"

"I don't know, Mom. We'll have to wait and see."

My files may be gone?

Rick saw the horror on my face and tried to cheer me up. "You've had this computer at least five years! That's a long time."

Five years? A long time? Rick is telling me, born during the Great Depression, how long things last? That five years is a good life for a computer? Now I'd need to purchase a "bigger, better, newer" one at a higher cost. And it would have a different program I'd have to learn. Would people buy new cars if they had to learn to drive all over again? The "old" computer was headed for the dump. Oops... I mean the politically correct "landfill."

In the years after the Depression, people were cautious with what they threw in the trash. Nothing was ever discarded. If something broke, there was always someone who could fix it. Remember Mr. Bob? His shop was just down the hill. He fixed irons and toasters and radios, usually for fifty cents. He wouldn't be able to stay in business today. We throw everything away.

There were no single-service items such as paper towels, paper napkins, paper cups and on and on. Only when people had a little more discretionary income did disposable products hit the shelves. People began buying single-use sanitary napkins, rolled paper towels, tissues... Our landfills are full, our air and water foul.

Automobiles are disposable as well. Home tinkerers and garage mechanics used to get 100,000 miles out of a car and then coax another 50,000 out of the old engine. Today? Forget the home tinkerer. A mechanic needs to know as much about computers as engines.

Now I have the use of a brand new laptop. It's sleek and flashy, and I don't like it. The piece I was writing for this week is gone! It disappeared. We looked everywhere and finally found a bit of it in the recycle bin. *How did it get there? I didn't put it there. Or did I? Did I hit a wrong key?*

I don't like all these new machines that are supposed to help us: the washer, the dryer, the microwave, the copier, the scanner. They are not loyal. Each time one of them breaks down I feel responsible and ungrateful. I also get unreasonably angry.

Just give me an old Royal and a clothesline.

THE GOOD OLD DAYS

Gas was 25 cents a gallon. We'd pull up to the tank and my grandfather would say, "Two dollars, please." The attendant would pump the gas AND check the oil and water AND wash the windshield.

Phone calls didn't start with an impersonal dial tone. The operator said "Number, please." If the call could not be completed, she said, "The line is busy" or "There is no answer." You said, "Thank you." She said, "You're welcome."

Wonder Bread cost a dollar for three loaves. Three pounds of hamburger meat sold for a dollar and so did bananas. Milk was 20 cents a quart.

Children played outdoors. They talked to each other. They looked you in the eye when they spoke to you. They said "please" and "thank you." Boys didn't wear hats indoors and stood when a lady entered the room. They wore trousers belted around their waists. Girls wore dresses.

Flags flew on Flag Day and Memorial Day and the other official flag flying days. Stores were closed on Memorial Day.

Men would walk or drive the short distance to work. There were no long commutes. Children walked to neighborhood schools. Women had dinner on the table when "the man" came home. Everyone "washed up" before coming to the table. This was a time for talking about the day or the world, with information gathered from the radio and newspaper. There were no dishwashers. Mothers washed dishes and children took turns drying. After dinner, people talked to each other, read, played board games and enjoyed their families.

Women wrung clothes in the washing machine's wringer attachment. Clothes were hung on a line outside to dry. In the winter and on rainy days, they were hung in the basement.

Airplanes were available for distant travel. But trains were the way to go for the faint of heart.

National election results were not known until the next day. California was not disenfranchised by knowing the presumed winner before their polls closed. West coast voters cast their votes and they meant something.

Television was in its infancy. Screens were perhaps five or six inches square. Prizefights and test patterns were the viewing choices.

Communication was slow and local. We were not burdened with disappearances in Aruba or bombarded with news of revolutions in small countries. Our hearts were not heavy with stories about earthquakes and famines, in which babies died by the thousands. We were not assaulted by vivid sexual scenes or irresponsible violence in movies.

Sex was personal. Divorce was nobody's business but the couple involved. Incest and child abuse were hidden within the family. Domestic abuse was suffered in silence. We had the Ku Klux Klan, the War to End All Wars and the atomic bomb.

Ah, those were the "good old days." Some of those days were not good at all. But some of them were swell.

VOICEMAIL

The voicemail plague began in 1898 with the patent of the Telegraphone. Its purpose was to record telephone conversations.

I remember my first encounter with an answering machine many years ago. I left a message as directed, but I was angry. I was no longer in control. I liked the old days when the phone rang and rang until I knew no one was home. I could call again at *my* convenience. Now I had to wait for my friend to call back.

The first home answering machine was bulky and awkward to use. But we put up with the inconvenience for the convenience of being available every moment of our lives.

Today we have voicemail; no more bulky appliances. The works have been minimized to a small chip that fits in your telephone. Even the smallest cell phone receives voicemail. You may now obtain the service directly from the telephone company, in which case, a startling staccato dial tone lets you know you have a message.

Is all this necessary? I don't think so. I do not need to know the moment Janie's cat is visually pregnant. I am not interested in the telemarketer's message that he has an insurance plan designed especially for me.

Did you know your computer can be your voicemail gatherer? Check the internet for instructions. Now that the computer and voicemail have teamed up, we will never have private, quiet time again.

Then there are family messages like this one from Cathy, my 16-year old: "Hi, Mom, I'm going to Janie's after school. I won't be home for dinner." or "Hi, honey. I have a new out-of-town client who's staying at the hotel. I told him it would be fine for him to come for dinner tonight. We'll see you soon." Well, at least I won't have to put out another chair – Cathy won't be here. The problem with voicemail: the caller thinks leaving the message is permission.

There are also hysterical messages from member organizations like the PTA. "Marsha, we don't have enough baked goods for the bazaar. Please bake another cake."

Ah, the outgoing message. Worried about creating a memorable one? There are more than several websites that offer "humorous" outgoing messages. In your search engine enter 'funny outgoing voice mail messages' or, 'outgoing voice mail messages'. Some are free, some you pay for.

Hi! John's answering machine is broken. This is his refrigerator. Please speak very slowly, and I'll stick your message to myself with one of these magnets.

My personal outgoing message? "Just do it."

UNITED STATES POSTAL SERVICE

The Postal Creed, familiar to all of us, reads as follows:

Neither snow, nor rain, nor heat, nor gloom of night, stays these couriers from the swift completion of their appointed rounds.

The words are from the works of Herodotus, dated about 500 B.C. The Persians operated a system of mounted postal couriers, and the quote describes the fidelity with which their work was performed.

As of August 2013, letters will no longer be delivered to your home or business on Saturdays. Post Office Boxes will still be filled. Packages and Priority Mail will be delivered. But Saturday sorting of the mail will be discontinued. What does that mean for Monday deliveries?

When I was a youngster, mail came Monday through Saturday *twice a day, six days a week.* At ten in the morning and three in the afternoon the mailman – there were no mailwomen – would knock on the door and call out, "Mail's here. You got a letter from your son, and your sisters are having a swell time in Atlantic City. You got your electric bill, too."

Grandma would go to the door and get the mail. Depending upon the season, she would invite Bob in for hot coffee or cool lemonade. They would talk about their families, politics and other peoples' mail.

The day came when Saturday afternoon delivery was cancelled. Three o'clock on Saturdays was a mournful hour. It took a long time to become accustomed to one less delivery. So imagine the national brouhaha when the Monday-through-Friday afternoon deliveries were cancelled.

And now, no Saturday delivery. This action is being taken to help solve financial problems.

Mail carriers now work five days a week so I do not see this as a money saver. They can still work five days and have the weekend off. A skeleton crew will still be needed on Saturdays to deliver packages and priority mail. It is estimated that a billion dollars will be saved in fuel costs and another billion dollars in manpower. Not nearly enough to get the United States Postal Service out of its fiscal jam.

The post office delivers to *every* residence and business in the United States in some manner. These days, only 25% of postal recipients receive their mail at the door. The rest now get their mail in cluster boxes, P.O. boxes, or at the curb. This change is estimated to save $5 billion dollars a year.

Still, the Postal Service currently spends $25 billion dollars to deliver mail directly to more than 150 million homes and businesses. It would be cheaper if all mail receptacles were in a centralized location, such as a neighborhood cluster box. But still not enough to solve USPS fiscal problems. This is one factor cited by those who'd like to give a green light to privatization of the nation's mail delivery.

According to a USPS spokesperson, the real financial problem now facing the post office comes from a 2006 Congressional mandate. This mandate requires the agency to "pre-pay" into a fund that covers health care costs for future retired employees. Under the mandate, the USPS is required to make an annual $5.5 billion dollar payment over ten years, through 2016. These "prepayments" are largely responsible for the USPS financial losses. The threat of shutdown looms ahead. Take the retirement fund out of the equation, and the postal service would have actually netted $1 billion dollars in profits over this period.

This reserve is not demanded of any government agency or private sector corporation. Looks like another green light. No wonder the USPS is in financial straits.

The post office is doing a thriving business in forever stamps. Buy forever stamps today at 46 cents and you can use that stamp forever to send your mail. Individuals and businesses buy thousands at a time. Will a private corporation honor them?

USPS takes a letter from Alaska to Hawaii for 46 cents. Will a private corporation do that?

FedEx and UPS now rely on the post office for delivery to remote areas. Will these addresses get their mail if privatization becomes a reality?

The post office has often been accused of shoddy accounting. An example: The USPS made an over payment of $11 billion dollars* to a government pension fund. The Postal Service has asked that the money be returned. The Senate has approved the request. The House will not hear it until sometime next year, perhaps too late to allow continued operation of the USPS.

According to POSTAL FACTS, "The USPS is not a government-owned corporation, but an independent establishment of the Executive Branch of the United States responsible for providing postal service." Policies and decisions are made by Congress, yet *no tax dollars are allocated to the operation of the USPS.*

If annual payments for the health plan are cancelled or lowered and the $11 billion dollar over payment is returned, the post office will be in the black.

The United States Postal Service has delivered our mail since 1893. Don't stop them now.

*In researching for this article, I found several dollar amounts for the overpayment. The number most frequently mentioned was $11 billion.

MARRIAGE:
It Isn't What It Used to Be

The water, just a drop hotter than warm, cascaded over my tense body. The shower spray was set on low massage. I luxuriated in my solitude within the walls of glass. Then suddenly, the water ran cold.

Damn him. I told him I was taking a shower. He must have turned on the hot water in the kitchen. Like my marriage, hot at first, now icy cold.

The water swirled down the drain.

Being married is not what it used to be. It used to be a commitment. Not anymore. The late Margaret Mead said, "Marriage isn't obsolete ... it's what we expect of it. Two people can't be all things to each other all the time."

Yet people keep trying. Attempts to live together range from fragile to frivolous, funny to futile.

Getting married was, at one time, an obligation to our families and to society. "Going steady" in high school had the wedding as its goal. It's not like that any more. *My teen-age son tells me he belongs to a Pokeher Club. There are six members and the object is to see how many girls they can bed in a month. The winner gets a pizza party in his honor.*

Couples often stayed together for the sake of the children.

One couple in their nineties went to their attorney seeking a divorce. They had been married more than seventy years. The attorney asked if they had always been unhappy. The man said yes. "Why did you wait until now for a divorce?" questioned the attorney. The woman answered. "We were waiting for the children to die."

Today, marriages that appear to have the best chance of success are "fun" marriages. The match is based on living "the good life." All flash, no glowing embers. If the people involved don't derive personal satisfaction and "fun" from the marriage, they want out.

Technology has made it easier for people to live alone. Men no longer need women to look after their daily-living needs. Convenience foods, the microwave and easy-care clothing have cut down on personal maintenance. Women, encouraged in careers, have found they too can make it by themselves. Gays who found marriage to a straight person a safe closet in which to hide are opening the door.

The role models of yesteryear are irrelevant. Today's marriage is a completely new phenomenon. More than 50% of marriages end in divorce. The percentage is higher in second marriages.

The trick is to avoid slipping on the residue as your marriage goes down the drain.

THE FAMILY DOCTOR

Dr. Tenke brought most of the kids in my school into the world. He even delivered some of their parents. He didn't deliver me because I was twelve when I moved to Glen Cove. I had been living with my grandparents. When they died, I came to live with Aunt Anne, Uncle Lou and my cousins, Mara and Harvey.

I became one of the family, right down to Dr. Tenke, who was the family doctor. He remained my doctor until after I was married. Then he became "our doctor".

Cousin Mara was terrified of shots. One day she had a terrible flu and Aunt Anne called Dr. Tenke to come to the house. Some doctors still made house calls and Dr. Tenke was one of them. Mara looked at him with a scared rabbit sort of stare. He took her temperature. One hundred three point five, he announced.

Knowing Mara's dreadful fear of shots, Dr. Tenke said, "Well, Mara, you can have your shot here or you can go to the hospital and have it there. You might as well stay in the hospital for a few days while you're there."

Mara writhed out of bed and slithered out the open bathroom window onto the porch roof. Dr. Tenke went right out the window after her. That was typical behavior for our family doctor. He grabbed her and jammed the needle right into

Mara's upper arm. They both climbed back through the window, Dr. Tenke helping Mara like the gentleman he was: Mara pushing him away and crying.

Then there was the time I went to see him a few months after I was married. I thought I might be pregnant. Those were the years of rabbit tests. Urine from the woman was injected into a rabbit. The rabbit's death confirmed pregnancy.

"So, Dr. Tenke, I'd like a rabbit test," I said.

He asked when I had my last period. I told him. He grabbed his pen and did a little calculating, squeezed my ankles and said, "Hell's Bells, why do you want to kill a rabbit? You're going to have a baby on April 28th." And I did.

I miss Dr. Tenke. We don't have family doctors today. We have Primary Care Physicians (PCP). They don't have roll top desks with the top open and files filled with papers sticking out every which way. Primary Care Physicians have computers and spend the entire appointment reading the screen or inputting information. There's little eye-to-eye contact between patient and doctor.

The PCP appointment is booked for fifteen minutes – a time strictly adhered to. It took Dr. Tenke fifteen minutes just to ask about the rest of the family. Then he'd want to know how my headaches were doing. Finally, his feet on the desktop and leaning back in his chair, Dr. Tenke would ask me about the current ailment. He was in no hurry. He knew the waiting room was full, but each of his patients would get the same personal care, the same attention.

Office hours started at eight in the morning. Dr. Tenke was often late. He had already been out on house calls. The doctor was completely unaware of meal times. The office did not close for lunch. Most days, Mrs. Tenke brought a lunch tray to the office. Often, she brought two trays, one for the patient. Emergencies were handled by Dr. Tenke, usually within minutes. The PCP's voice mail tells you to call 911.

So many differences between the family doctor and the Primary Care Physician – like capitalizing Physician and not doctor.

We miss you, Dr. Tenke.

POSSLQ

We just had the big 2010 Decennial Census. So we're done for now, right? The Census Department gets to take a vacation until 2020?

No way. There are annual studies, five-year studies and my favorite, the Adirondack Loon Census. It is done on the third Saturday of each July with the help of the Wildlife Conservation Society.

Every once in a while, the Census discovers a statistic they don't know what to do with. Like POSSLQ (poss-ell-que), an acronym for "persons of opposite sex sharing living quarters." Usually this living arrangement was not planned and seemed to "just happen." First the toothbrush, then the razor, then the extra shirt in the closet. Then the realization that it's silly to maintain two residences.

It was in the 1960s that this pattern began evolving. There was an increasing frequency of cohabitation. The old method of counting cohabiters involved a series of complicated assumptions because of "in the closet" questions.

What used to be called "living in sin" has now been okayed by the Census Bureau! The category "unmarried partner" first appeared in the 1990 Census. By the late 1990s, POSSLQ had fallen out of general use except for demographers and CBS commentator Charles Osgood, who composed the following verse:

There's nothing that I wouldn't do
If you would be my POSSLQ.
You live with me and I with you,
And you will be my POSSLQ.
I'll be your friend and so much more;
That's what a POSSLQ is for.

THE NEW FAMILY

Part One

Liz and Kate had lived together for almost nine years when Liz announced she wanted a baby. Kate agreed.The family, it's a-changin'.

In the old days, the *extended family* consisted of parents, children, and other close relatives, usually three generations, living in the same home or in close proximity. The *nuclear family* developed early in the 19th century when industry became our major source of employment. It consisted of wife/mother, husband/father and their children, and quickly outnumbered the extended family.

The family farm and the Mom-and-Pop store were fading from the scene. There was no back forty to plow and Woolworth's was nudging the family store from its corner. Members of the nuclear family followed their employers to wherever the work was. It was easier to move Mom, Dad and the kids than to get three generations of kinfolk on the road. Independent of all those extra relatives, the nuclear unit fit the needs of an industrial society and was free to move as the economy demanded.

Most of us grew up thinking the nuclear family was the only normal, natural family. This has had a profound influence on research, therapy, and public policy. Any departure from the nuclear family is considered unhealthy and/or immoral.

Well, hold on, folks. There are other families on the block.

Today, there are many forms of family units, and they are quickly outpacing nuclear families. They include households with a single mother, single father, two moms or two dads.

Let me tell you about a non-nuclear family I recently visited.

Part Two

Liz and Kate looked at all the pros and cons. They decided there were more yeas than nays for a two-mommy household. And so it began, as it does for every couple facing parenthood. Decisions had to be made.

Housing: Liz and Kate had purchased property, including a three-story house in a neighborhood ideal for children. There was a small, fenced back yard, a front porch with rocking chairs, and a huge park, the length of the block, right across the street.

Who's Who? What do you call two mommies? Mommy One and Mommy Two? I don't think so. They decided that every time they interacted with the baby, they'd say, Hi, here's Mommy Liz or Mommy Kate.

<u>School</u>: The house was in a good school district. They'd have to check on nursery schools and register the baby immediately.

<u>The Legalities</u>: Liz is the biological mother. This whole baby thing was her idea anyway. Kate would legally adopt the baby, sharing the financial burden, life planning and the daily responsibilities involved in child rearing.

<u>What about Dad</u>? They needed to find a biological dad. Liz and Kate agreed that two people making decisions, planning and disciplining the child were quite enough. They would have a legal agreement drawn up for the dad to sign. The father would have no rights to the baby, bear no financial responsibility and have no voice in life planning. He would provide the sperm that would impregnate Liz. He must be a superlatively healthy person: very smart, good genes, and a great sense of humor.

In addition, he must sign that agreement.

The hunt was on for Bio Dad.

Part Three

Early on, Liz and Kate decided not to go to a sperm bank. They had heard rumors that not all men answered the questionnaires truthfully.

The women checked lists of acquaintances independently and both came up with the same name. Now, if he would just agree to father their child.

Liz and Kate invited Robbie to dinner. After a delicious meal of braised spare ribs and parsnips, Liz popped the question.

"Robbie, Kate and I are planning to have a baby and we'd like you to be the biological father."

Robbie picked up his jaw from the table.

Kate spoke next. "Liz will be the biological mom and I'm going to adopt the baby. We have a paper for the Bio Dad to sign. Here, read this." Kate handed 'the paper' to Robbie.

So far, not a word from Robbie. But his body language expressed his interest.

Liz chimed in, "I hope you'll do it, Robbie. We want the dad to be a real dad, in spite of what that paper says. We want to have a feeling of family and the baby to know who his dad is. But we want to take care of the baby ourselves financially and make life decisions. It just gets too complicated with a lot of people."

Robbie looked at Liz and then at Kate, wearing a small half-grin and smiling eyes. "I'd be honored, ladies," he said with a little bow.

Liz, Kate and Robbie went through the pregnancy together: the nausea, the backaches, the leg cramps and, although minimal, the weight gain. Kate and Robbie were both in the delivery room during Liz's labor and saw Baby Eve's little head pop into the world.

This is a story about a family made up of non-traditional people, or so you may think. This family is far more typical than you may imagine.

Liz is a medical doctor in charge of a government methadone clinic. She also has a Ph.D. in etymology research.

Kate has her MBA. She is in upper management in a leading Canadian bank group and is next in line for a vice-presidency.

Robbie also has an MBA and works at finding funding for major motion pictures. This year, not for the first time, one of his films is nominated in several categories in the Oscar competition.

Three Years Later

This is a story of love – so much love that it is higher than the sky and wider than water where there is no other side.

Eve is smart, well adjusted, funny and tall.

Robbie and Eve go swimming every Saturday and have dinner together every Sunday at Robbie's condo. They talk on the phone during the week and sometimes have surprise outings.

Eve loves her two mommies. Her two mommies love her and each brings to the child a very special part of herself.

There are three sets of doting grandparents, all of whom play a major part in Eve's life.

Traditions have been established. Christmas is spent at Robbie's parents' vacation cottage with Robbie, Eve and the mommies. Summer vacations include Robbie, the mommies and Eve. Liz's parents visit several times a year, as do Kate's.

February 15, 2011, 5:00 a.m. Jon was born at home. Robbie and Liz are his biological parents. The delivery room, again, was crowded ... this time celebrating the arrival of Eve's biological brother.

Changing Places

We may not remember where we've been,
we may not know where we are,
but we are always somewhere.

The Early Years
The Martha Washington Hotel for Women
New Orleans
Key West 1981
Santeria
The Doll
The Candidate
With Egrets: Florida, 50 Years Ago
The Tour Director
On the Way to Antarctica

THE EARLY YEARS

I was brought home from the hospital to a ten-room apartment above GeeGee's furniture store in Floral Park, Long Island. My parents lived there with Bubby and GeeGee. It had plenty of bathrooms. Usually wherever you lived back then, there was only one bathroom. We were lucky; we had three. What did I care? I wasn't even potty trained.

Bubby and GeeGee were my mother's parents. Uncle Mitt and Aunt Anne were her siblings. Uncle Mitt lived with us in the apartment. Aunt Anne lived in Glen Cove with her husband and children. They came to visit often.

My mom and dad opened a chain of 16 shoe repair shops. Remember, this was in the days when people had their shoes re-soled and re-heeled. When my parents were away on business, Bubby looked after me. She was short and round and had the squishiest bosom where I could rest my head anytime I needed comforting.

My mom died when I was a year old but her death did not really affect me. Then my dad died when I was three. Again, I didn't feel any difference. I was still living in the same place with the same people. My favorite places in the whole world were Bubby's and GeeGee's laps. I felt so loved and comfortable. My, they were good to me.

GeeGee and Bubby would think of ways to entertain me. I would hear the call, "Let's go have some fun," and I'd come running. GeeGee took me anywhere he thought I'd like to go. They didn't want me to miss a thing. I was spoiled and stubborn.

GeeGee took me to the Ringling Bros. Circus in Madison Square Garden when I was four. He bought one seat. Not because he was cheap, but because he knew this would be the biggest, most crowded, noisiest place I had ever been. He knew how safe I felt on his lap. We got to the Garden. I saw we had only one seat and I wanted my own chair. I stood with my back to the excitement in the three rings for the entire circus, pouting. I was a good pouter.

People were knitting hats and mufflers to send to England for the Red Cross. I could make only potholders and I couldn't really knit; I purled. The Red Cross lady didn't want to discourage me; she always picked up my potholders. If they got to England, there must have been some surprised faces over there. Maybe they're still in a Red Cross warehouse somewhere.

The years passed and it was time to start school. I walked back and forth each day, whistling as I hiked the half mile each way. I don't remember kindergarten. Perhaps in those years, school started in grade one.

Miss Abraham was my first grade teacher. She had black curly hair and she was t-i-n-y. A couple of the boys were almost taller than she was. Could she have been a "little person?" Not in those days; she would have been a midget.

It was in the second grade I realized I was different. I didn't have a mother to help with the bake sale. Bubby baked better than anyone else, and I am ashamed to say this: I did not want Bubby to *be* there, with her accent and her braided gray hair coiled around her head. None of the mothers had gray hair or spoke with an accent.

On Mothers' and Fathers' Days, I wore a white carnation because my parents were dead. Pink carnations were for those who had living parents. On the following Mondays, everyone else came to school wearing their pink flowers. Those carnations caused an inexplicable pain in what I now know is my heart.

School was uneventful until the day I used the "F" word in the cafeteria. I have no idea where I heard it and had no idea what the word meant. Bubby and GeeGee had to come to school to take me home. They did not know what the word meant either. I was in the fifth grade when Bubby and a neighbor sat me down on the couch to teach me the facts of life. This consisted of, "Don't ever let a boy touch you."

Louie was the biggest bully in school. When he cut ahead of me in the lunch line, I poured a bowl of hot tomato soup over his head. Another trip to school for Bubby and GeeGee.

These trips were difficult for them. GeeGee's English wasn't bad. He needed to learn the language quickly to run his business. However, Bubby did not get out much, so we decided we would spend an hour each day and I would teach her English. We sat down at the kitchen table every night at 7:00 PM. We never missed a night. Within six months, Bubby was speaking English, albeit with an accent, and learning to read and write. Bubby was a quick learner and rapidly achieved her goal. She became an American citizen.

We had a huge porch over the downstairs storeroom. A white railing ran around it. Every afternoon at 4:00, I would stand at the rail and belt my little heart out. I loved to sing; I knew all the oldies and the war songs. Occasionally a few people would gather on the sidewalk below, some to cheer, some to jeer. I didn't care either way. I just kept singing.

We lived near Mitchell Field, a major air force base. Someone from the USO called GeeGee and asked if I would sing "for the boys." How did they know I loved to sing? It was 1942, a year into the war. I was eight years old. We were invited back a bunch of times. Maybe I reminded "the boys" of their kid sisters back home. Maybe they liked the song they requested most often. I just recently realized "Rum and Coca Cola" verged on the bawdy... "Both mothah and daughtah workin' for the Yankee Dollah."

I was ten when Gil and Rose Mack came into my life. We went to the same synagogue and I did a recitation for one of the holidays. They thought I had "talent." Gil was the busiest, most successful radio actor in the business. Television was still mostly the Test Pattern and an occasional boxing match. Rose was a sought-after diction tutor. They asked Bubby and GeeGee if I could come to their house Saturday mornings for acting lessons.

For two years, I visited them every Saturday. First, I would meet with Rose and she taught me the phonetic alphabet and proper diction. So why do I still say Longg Island and Noo Yawk?

Gil would bring scripts from all his shows for that week. He'd assign a part and teach me how to mark the script. *Then we would Act.* The Macks were certain I would be a big star. I hoped I would. We had publicity photos taken and I needed to choose my stage name. Showbiz names needed to sound "all American." Archie Leach became Cary Grant. Marsha Wernicoff was not going to cut it. The first name I chose was Daff O'Dill. Gil quickly talked me out of that one. My middle name is Idelle – I became Idelle Marsh, had stationery and business cards printed.
Gil took me into the city for some of his shows. I loved the live spontaneity of it all. No one knew anything about taping back then.

One day we all came out of the studio. There were some stars on the show. A crowd had gathered outside asking for autographs. One of them asked me; I signed, "Happy Life, Idelle Marsh." He said, "Who are you?" and I started to laugh. First, because of his question and second, because my name sounded like Mish Mahsh.

I kept the name and volunteered for the American Theater Wing in 1945. I was eleven years old. During WW II, the Wing provided much of the entertainment available to the troops, including the Stage Door Canteen. After the war, the Wing was part of the G.I. Bill. Veterans who chose to be actors, producers, directors, lighting specialists – anything stagecraft related – studied at the Wing. This was where I volunteered, working with those interested in radio acting. Today, the American Theater Wing is responsible for choosing and presenting the Tonys for Excellence in the Theatre. The presentations are televised every year.

Was I one lucky kid, or what?

THE MARTHA WASHINGTON HOTEL FOR WOMEN

This was the winter of my discontent, cold and icy. I was bored with the sameness of Glen Cove. I wanted to move to Manhattan, see the shows, meet some interesting people for a change. But I would need to convince Aunt Anne.

"New York? You want to move to New York? You are just a child! How can you move to New York by yourself?"

"Aunt Anne, I'll be eighteen in a few days. I'll be in my room by dark, except for school nights, and the subway is almost at the front door of the hotel I found."

"Hotel? You found a hotel? Why is *this* hotel okay?" asked Aunt Anne, furiously fanning herself with a *New Yorker* magazine.

"It's the Martha Washington Hotel for Women. It opened in 1903 and was the first hotel exclusively for women. A man has never gotten in the elevator or up the stairs in all those years. And, it's on the East Side." That should be the clincher. The East Side was the best side of New York, according to Aunt Anne.

"Well, let's go into the city Saturday and have a look at this place."

Saturday we took the Long Island Railroad to Pennsylvania Station. We walked the couple of blocks to the hotel on East 30th Street, a very safe neighborhood in 1950.

When we got to the hotel, High Tea was being served in the lobby. The residents were wearing their hats and gloves, daintily sipping tea. I blinked and looked again. There was not a person there who was under eighty! *Today we would call it assisted living, except there were no wheelchairs or walkers.* These women were wealthy dowagers who had outlived their husbands and were enjoying a pleasant life of shopping, theater and High Tea.

At the front desk, Aunt Anne asked to see a typical room.

"Oh, I know you would be very comfortable here, madam."

"It's for my niece," said my aunt frigidly.

The desk clerk wisely said no more and dinged her little bell. A trim woman in a neat uniform of white blouse and dark skirt answered the call to take us on a tour. As we walked by the Tea, our guide told us it was served every day at four. Then she showed us the coffee shop, the little sundries shop, the dining room (where men could dine if accompanied by a resident), and the bar. *The bar?!? Don't show Aunt Anne the bar! However, Aunt Anne appeared to be nonplussed. Thank you, Martha Washington, Protector of Women.*

Our guide, whose name was Tess, walked us to the old-fashioned elevator with the sliding brass gate. The elevator operator wore the same uniform as Tess, except her blouse was sort of a dusty rust color. We got off on the ninth floor.

"This room is typical, and available," said Tess.

My fingers didn't touch the walls when I spread my arms but the room was pretty small. It was furnished with a twin-sized bed, a bedside table with lamp, a desk with telephone, a bureau and mirror and an easy chair. A light fixture, flush to the ceiling, lit the room. The silk carpet, obviously once expensive, must have been put down in 1903. There was a small closet and a tiny bathroom with a sink and toilet. The window looked out over busy East 30th Street.

And that was it.

Tess said, "The linens are changed and new towels delivered every Wednesday. This room is cleaned every Monday and Thursday."

"Tess, did we miss the tub and the shower?"

"No, they're out in the hall. Six rooms share them."

"I don't think I can do that, Tess."

"Don't worry, Miss Marsha, you'll learn the schedule. Besides, most of our people don't bathe every day."

We looked at the bathrooms. We looked at each other and Aunt Anne nodded her head. I could have flown down the nine flights. We thanked Tess and gave her a tip for the tour. I realized I'd have to factor tips into my budget.

I registered at the front desk and gave Aunt Anne a big hug.

The train ride home was a magic carpet. My belongings didn't take long to pack and I was back at the hotel on Monday.

My days quickly fell into a pattern. I had breakfast at the coffee shop in the lobby, and lunch would be the Tea where I met my geriatric neighbors. This was truly a den of antiquity. The ladies were good to me and were interested in my young life. They questioned me each day. "Who was that young man last night?" "Did you have your breakfast, dear?" The hotel had 416 rooms and I had 415 mothers.

Every day except Wednesday, after breakfast, I would ride the subway to a different neighborhood. I went everywhere from Harlem to Riverside Drive to Greenwich Village. I went to Mott Street, Pitkin Avenue and Mulberry Street. On Wednesdays, I went to matinees on and off Broadway.

Three nights a week, I attended a drama program at New York University. I met a man from Canada who had been at the Academy for Dramatic Arts on a fencing scholarship. What could be more romantic than a foreigner and a bladesman?

Aunt Anne asked, "A Canadian? A fencer? Is he at least Jewish?"

I checked into the Martha Washington Hotel for Women in January and checked out in May, when I married the Jewish Canadian Fencer.

Which surprised even me.

NEW ORLEANS

Part One

I was closing my apartment and putting everything in storage when the phone rang. It was a friend of a friend. I knew Dale, but not very well. I did know he was a successful CPA, specializing in IRS tax cases. He also had irons in many fires.

"How yuh doin'? Harl tells me you're closing your apartment and looking for an interesting place to go. How about New Orleans? I've got a business there and I fired my manager. You can do it. I'd really like you to do it."

"Whoa, Dale, slow down. What kind of business? I've never been in New Orleans. How soon do you need someone?"

"Now! I need somebody now! There's a plane from MIA in two hours. Can you make it? You can just check out the business and the town and come back tomorrow on a late flight. How about it?"

"Okay. I can be ready in a half hour. I'll be downstairs."

Well, Marsha, what have you gotten yourself into now? Oh well, it'll be fun to see New Orleans and if I don't like the whole thing, I'll be home tomorrow. I threw a change of clothes and underwear, deodorant, a toothbrush and toothpaste into a small case. A comb and some makeup went into my purse and I was ready to go.

We got to the airport, barely on time, and plopped down in the first-class seats Dale had booked. I took a deep breath and Dale launched into a description of his business that lasted the entire flight.

"It's in the middle block of Bourbon Street, best location in the Quarter." *I'm becoming interested. That is the French Quarter, also known as the Vieux Carré. I've always wanted to go there.*

"Here's the business in a nutshell. It's the Olde Tyme Costume Shop with old time costumes that tie in the back. From the front, the customer looks like an Old West cowboy, a pirate, a gay-ninety's dance girl or whatever. When you come in, you see the costumes and the old-fashioned box cameras. The trick is to get the folks to pick out costumes to wear. They can walk around on Bourbon Street for a while in costume and when they come back, we take their old-fashioned sepia picture. They just come in, right off of Bourbon Street. I've got two kids in there now. Cissy is 22 and Jeff is 23. They're good kids, but they can't handle the other business." *The other business? What other business? I'm beginning to worry.*

"The main business is selling time-shares. If a couple buys one, they get a free signed lithograph by Ferdie Pacheco. Know who he is?"

"No, I have no idea."

"No idea? He was only Mohammed Ali's personal medical doctor for years, in the ring and out. He was also boxing analyst for Showtime and a heck of an artist. We have low numbered, signed lithographs of all his work and buyers can choose whichever one they want. But the two businesses aren't merging the way they should. The old manager didn't do it. For sure, the kids can't do it. But I know you can. You understand people, you have the imagination and I know you'll put it all together."

"I think I understand it now, Dale. I'll think about it. I'm going to close my eyes for a while."

Dale kept talking till we landed. I dozed off.

We took a cab to the shop. To my surprise, it was the bottom floor of a typical French Quarter townhouse, three stories high, frosted with rococo wrought iron and balconies.

Casually, Dale said, "The whole building's yours. You'll have to decorate the two top floors. About the staff, you can hire and fire as many people as you want. Figure out the hours you want to be open. Don't forget to decorate – make it luxurious."

Cissy and Jeff were delightful Orleanians. Right off the bat I decided to keep them. *Keep them? I haven't decided to take the job. I'll look at the rest of the house and we'll take a walk. Then I'll decide. Who was I kidding? Something was holding me back from accepting immediately.*

The shop was clean and self-explanatory, so Dale and I went upstairs. The living room and bedroom were huge. The kitchen was a modern marvel and the bathroom was right out of *Architectural Digest*. The third floor contained two large bedrooms and a decent bathroom. One of the bedrooms was used for the storage of costumes, props and lots of rifles, sabers and swords.

I told Dale it was time for a walk. I was eager to see what kind of neighborhood I might be moving to.

The Quarter was a bouillabaisse of French and Spanish culture stirred together into a liberal way of life. Bourbon Street was a hodge-podge of smells, sights, sounds and people. Everyone appeared to be accepting and accepted. Local and tourist, gay and straight, black and white, young and old, all walked harmoniously on a street empty of traffic at night.

Music wailed out of open café doors – jazz and blues, trumpets and saxophones. Al Hirt's club was on the corner and Pete Fountain played his clarinet up the street. Preservation Hall was around the corner. Dale seemed to be involved with the Hall in some way. He told me I could go there whenever I wanted to and I could bring friends. Same at Al Hirt's. The locals seemed to know Dale. I guessed he was 'the man,' although I didn't really know what that meant.

We turned another corner onto Royal Street. People were window-shopping the profusion of magnificent antiques in the stores that lined the street. They'd be back tomorrow when this became a mall and the auto traffic was transferred to Bourbon Street for the daylight hours.

Back on Bourbon Street we had street food for dinner. Oyster Po'Boys and imported beer hit the spot. We walked some more until I started limping and took off my shoes. Then I started to yawn. Dale finally recognized the signs. He steered us to the hotel and we registered in the two rooms he had reserved. He left noon wake-up calls for both rooms. I was asleep before my head hit the pillow.

We had crepes for breakfast and I thought it was time to talk about money.

"Well, I thought $450 a week and we pay for all food, whether you eat all your meals out or shop at the A&P," said Dale. "Doesn't matter to me. Of course, you don't have to pay for a place to stay. The whole townhouse is yours. You'll always have access to an open airline ticket so you can come and go as you please. I trust you'll have everything organized so you can do that. What do you think?"

"Sounds very generous to me, Dale. Let me put it in the hopper with everything else. Now, let's go see New Orleans."

We boarded the St. Charles streetcar and rode through the Garden District, home to elaborate mansions. We toured a cemetery and walked some crooked streets.

Back on Bourbon Street, we observed the shop routine for a couple of hours until it was time to leave for the airport. Late as usual, we collapsed in our comfortable seats.

Dale asked the question I expected, but was dreading. "Do you like the shop, the house, New Orleans? What do you think?"

"Dale, I'm not sure. I'll call you tomorrow."

The plane left the ground and headed south for Miami.

Part Two

The next morning I called Dale. "I'd love to take the job in New Orleans and I'd like the last flight out on Tuesday."

"Hey, that's great! I'll make your flight reservation and book a room at the hotel for you until you get some furniture in there."

"Dale, is there anything else I need to know? Anything you want to tell me about the business?"

"Nope. You'll figure it all out. Have a safe flight and I'll be there in a couple of weeks."

That was Sunday and I had a few things to look after, including turning off the electricity and phone, paying my final month's rent, emptying the refrigerator. I needed to call some friends and let the children know where they could reach me.

It was definitely time for me to follow my usual method of working myself out of a quandary. My grandmother used to tell me to "take a pencil to paper." This has stood me in good stead many times. I wrote, "The business is an Olde Tyme Costume Shop on Bourbon Street in New Orleans's French Quarter. However, the real moneymaking business is selling first-rate time-share units. The costume shop is a come-on."

Now I needed a list of what I had to do:

1. Establish hours of operation (noon to midnight?)
2. Furnish the town house (find high-end furniture rentals)
3. Talk with Cissy and Jeff (get their take on what's needed)
4. Do I need more employees?
5. Determine a method of merging the photo shop and time-shares

That seemed like enough for the first week.

I arrived in New Orleans late Tuesday night and went directly to the hotel. The yellow pages had columns of rental furniture. I knew I'd be okay with that. I called for an 8:00 room service breakfast and planned to be at the shop at 9:30 the next morning when it opened. Cissy, Jeff and I could have our talk. It probably wasn't too busy in the morning.

"Hi, good morning. Remember me? I was here with Dale last week. My name is Marsha."

Cissy: "Welcome back."

Jeff: "Good to see you again."

"We'll be working together and I need to know what you know and I need your ideas. What do you think about changing the hours the shop is open? Are you busy in the morning?"

Jeff pointed to the street. "There's nobody out there until at least noon."

"Then, should we open at noon?" I asked.

"That would be super," said Cissy. "I get so bored here in the morning."

"What about at night?" asked Jeff, really getting into it. "Sometimes they're so drunk late at night they don't know where they are or what they're doing," he continued.

"So what time should we close?"

"Midnight!" they both answered.

"I agree," I said. "From noon to midnight sounds good to me. Good decision. Thanks. You'll need a half-hour in the morning and night to set up and close down. That's thirteen hours a day, seven days a week. Do either of you know anyone who can work about thirty-five hours a week? You'll each need at least one day a week off and we need to train someone in case one of you can't come in one day."

Cissy and Jeff each knew 'someone who would be perfect.' I asked them to make interview appointments for Thursday. *Good, this is going well. We've determined our hours and realized we need another body in the shop. Now it's time for me to learn how to do what they do down here.*

"Are you able to start the new hours today?" Both nodded.

"It's only 10:15. Here's some money... Go have breakfast and be back in time to open. This afternoon, you can teach me to use the camera, develop the pictures and all about the costumes." Cissy and Jeff left.

I found the phone book and set up four appointments with furniture rental companies for the next day. They would look at the property and drive me to their showrooms.

I have an idea for bringing in business but I need to look at the costumes carefully, find a printer and hire two more people.

My thoughts were interrupted by a knocking at the shop door. A woman wearing a glaring white uniform was standing there. I opened the door.

"Who you?" she demanded. "Where Cissy and Jeff?"

There was another knock at the door. This time it was a clean-cut young man.

"Let him in, he work here, too."

So she works here. What does he do? Seems like everybody gets here at 10:30, whatever they do.

"My name's Bobby. Don't worry about a thing. Ralphie's outside making sure everything is copacetic."

Bobby, Ralphie, Cissy, Jeff, and I don't even know her name. Time to sort this out.

"Ma'am, I'm sorry, I don't know your name."

"I's Penelope and I's your maid. I'se here five hours every day 'cept Satiday and Sunday." I smiled and nodded.

"Bobby, what do you do here?"

"I'm a licensed real estate agent. Time-shares can be sold only by registered agents. That's me."

"And Ralphie, outside. What's his job?"

"To protect you, ma'am. He'll walk behind you every time you go out. He also watches the store and the house," said Bobby in a comforting tone. He had no idea he was frightening me.

"Okay. I'm happy to meet you all. My name is Marsha and I'm the new manager. Go ahead and do whatever it is you do and we'll have a meeting this afternoon. We can get to know each other and talk about any changes."

Off they went.

My first day at work and it was nothing like I expected. What other surprises are in store for me? Dale, there's so much you didn't tell me.

Part Three

N'Awlins – that's the way to say it if you live here, and I'd been living here for a month now. Penelope is the best maid and we have become friends. Bobby's happy because he's closing more deals.

He and I play gin rummy when things are slow. *I guess I owe him about two hundred dollars. Oh, well, I have no other expenses.*

Ralphie, who's 6'6" tall, has shoulders that are about that wide. I wish he'd walk with me, instead of behind me; he follows me wherever I go. But that's his job.

Cissy, Jeff and Darryl are doing well in the shop. Darryl fits right in with the rest of the crew. He was the first to interview for the job and I liked him immediately. They make their own shop schedule and it's always covered. The costumes are clean and pressed and the shop always looks neat. Noon to midnight are perfect hours.

Remember, I had an idea for merging the costume shop with the time-share business? Our two new employees, Mary Sue and Huey, wear the costumes on the street. They work from 4:00 until 11:30, daylight hours on Royal Street and nights on Bourbon, changing costumes three times a shift. They hand out coupons that offer a free photograph if the customer goes upstairs to listen to the spiel. I'm astonished at how many coupons come back to the shop.

Mary Sue has the deepest dimples and wears a flower in her short curly hair. Huey is part of the Huey Long family, as charming a scoundrel as all the rest of them with a southern accent that drips like molasses. I allow them to go out as a pair. Neither one of them is ever alone and they can't have Ralphie.

We were taking pictures and selling time-shares. Everything was going well. I had bruises on my knuckles from knocking on wood. My days fell into a delightful pattern of working and sightseeing. I ate at all the fine restaurants in the Quarter while Ralphie waited outside. His choice, not mine. Brennan's and a little crepe café around the corner were my favorites.

I had a nodding acquaintance with some of my neighbors. The tattooed spider man had a web that looked like it covered his entire body. The web finally disappeared up his left nostril. Mickey Strike was the size of a rotunda and is an international mask maker. He gets orders from all around the world.

Then there was the Bead Lady, a creepy unsmiling person, always dressed in a long, plain brown dress. Her eerie message was uttered through thin lips. "Buy a bead from me and you will have good luck." The inference, of course: if you didn't buy a bead you'd immediately fall down and break your skull. I bought a bead a day.

Weird things were happening. At night, I'd hear footsteps and voices coming from the first floor. I was the only person in the house at night. I called the police and they said there were 15 calls ahead of me. I asked if you had to take a number for help in N'Awlins. I'd put things down and they'd be moved. The phone would ring and no one would be there.

Dale came down about this time, for just one day. He said that he had many meetings with very important people and would use the office I had created upstairs. Swarthy men with heavy briefcases came to meet with Dale. When they left the briefcases swung light in their hands. This went on for two hours.

Then a hush fell over the townhouse. An elegantly dressed man with a vicuna coat over his shoulders came into the shop. Three other men whose eyes flew everywhere surrounded him. He asked if the office was upstairs. I watched four pair of feet climb the stairs, one pair clad in ostrich leather shoes. Obviously, this was the most important meeting of the day. *I look outside and there is the black Cadillac El Dorado I suspected would be there. The driver is having a friendly talk with Ralphie.*

DUH! I finally realize this whole thing – the costume shop, the time-shares – is a Laundromat. And not the kind that has a rinse cycle.

Dale and Ostrich Shoes came downstairs, whispering to each other. Dale introduced us. "Shoes" told me what a wonderful job I was doing and whatever I was earning, he was going to double it. *Now I know for sure this is not the Boy Scouts I'm involved with.*

Dale saw Shoes to his car with a diffidence I had never seen in him. I told Dale I'd like a meeting right now. He must have known what was coming.

"Now I recognize the nagging feeling I had when you approached me. Had I known for sure what it was, I'd have never accepted. It's not that I'm a puritan – I'm frightened."

"But I *gave* you Ralphie."

"*Ralphie* is a perfect example of what I'm afraid of. Kind and gentle one moment and a killing machine the next. I don't want to do this anymore." I brushed away a tear. "Dale, I'm leaving tomorrow morning. The business can run itself for as long as needed – and I'm proud of that."

The next day was Halloween, 1977. I had been in N'Awlins for a wonderful six months. It was a delightful experience, but now that my fears had been realized, I just couldn't stay any longer. Not even a day.

I sat in my comfortable first-class seat as the plane headed south for Miami.

KEY WEST 1981

Part One

An invisible hand pushed my little brown Pinto down Highway 1 to Key West, the southernmost point in the United States. I was headed toward the best ten years of my life. But what anguish I felt driving down. I hardly noticed the beauty that surrounded me.

It's 113 miles and 42 bridges from Miami-Dade County to Key West. *National Geographic* considers the Overseas Highway one of the world's greatest drives. U.S. 1 was built on some of the original railway spans of Henry Flagler's ill-fated railroad, on the coral bedrock of individual keys and on specially constructed columns. The highway was considered an engineering miracle when construction began in the late 1930s. It is still a remarkable road, with the Atlantic Ocean on the left and the Gulf of Mexico on the right. The waters turn from teal to aqua to a deep navy blue. Markers count the miles, ending in Key West at Mile Marker 0.

As I counted off the mile markers, I wondered what my life would be like on an island where I knew only one person. Luckily, Camille had invited me to stay on her houseboat for a few days. At least I wouldn't need to stay in a motel. But I needed to find a place to live. And I needed to find a job, quickly; my funds were running dangerously low.

The Miami-Key West trip took just under four hours and I was on Camille's boat by 5:00 PM. We went out for an early dinner and picked up a copy of the local newspaper. I checked the ads and found a little furnished conch house that looked interesting. I called and made an appointment for the morning.

The house had all the modern necessities, including window air conditioners. There were two bedrooms, living room, kitchen, one bath and a delightful garden at the back. It was furnished comfortably and charmingly, in not-very-valuable antiques. There was some nice wicker in the living room and a good old table and benches in the kitchen.

The house was perfect, right on Eaton Street, one of the main streets of Old Town... except it was far too much money. But I was certain I could get a roommate. *What was I thinking? A roommate? I'd never had a roommate in my life.*

I told the agent I'd take the house.

Now I needed a job *and* a roommate. I picked up the morning paper.

The local newspaper was *The Key West Citizen*, otherwise known as the Mullet Wrapper. The ink never seemed to dry completely and came off on the reader's hands – you always knew who'd read the paper that day. Facts were not always checked and often, the date on the masthead was wrong. It was to this paper I was entrusting my life.

I ran to the newspaper office, within easy walking distance from my new house, and met Liz, the Circulation Manager. She was from Scotland, and spoke with that delightful burr. We hit it off right away and I had a job!

I called the number in the roommate ad and spoke with Rob. We made an appointment for the same afternoon at Pepe's on Caroline Street. What a sweet person – 24 years old and two years left at mortician's school. *Mortician's school?* His dad was a mortician and so was his grandfather and, if Rob has children, they too will be morticians.

I remembered a Mortician's Convention in New Orleans. I'd had T-shirts made that said, "Put the Fun Back in Funerals." I wondered if Rob's dad had one.

Rob and I talked about the usual matters potential roommates talk about: respect, bathroom and kitchen conditions, guests, common areas and the dozen other things that need to be settled for a happy home. We found we were compatible. Rob would split the rent with me! I was moving in the next day and Rob would be there the following weekend.

I took a deep breath. In one day, I had found a job, a house and a roommate! I knew Key West was magic... but this was super magic. Powerful as a genie just released from his bottle.

Part Two

It took me no time to settle into Key West. The island itself is welcoming. Porches spill out to narrow lanes, eager to greet visitors. Greedy pelicans eat from your hand. Fragrant blossoms fill the air with their alluring scents. Banyan trees are deeply rooted in yesterday, their branches reaching for today. The people are smart, charming, talented and friendly.

From my vantage point at the *Key West Citizen*, I got to know many folks. I sat at the first desk and as people came in, mine was the first face they saw. There was always a smile and a hello. Thus was I introduced to the island residents.

Ted was the manager of a local radio station. I told him I had radio experience in New York. I wanted to do a human-interest program and would do it at no cost to the station. He said, "Great! Let's set up a time to talk about it. How's noon tomorrow?"

It was my turn to say, "Great." Then, "How about if I bring sandwiches for both of us to Fort Taylor? You bring the drinks."

It was a beautiful day. Not a cloud anywhere.

"I've got an opening at five in the morning. Want it?"

"Sure, Ted. I do the Suicide Hotline from six to seven. That's a perfect time."

"Okay, we're set. Just be there Sunday morning at quarter to five. There'll be a sound person there to work the board. And listen, you don't have to check with me first on anything. If you're doing wrong, you'll hear from me."

What a magical place. I pinched myself each day for reassurance. This was a BIG pinch.

One of the reporters wrote a column stating his opinion that men could easily get along without women. I wrote a Letter to the Editor saying women did not need men. My letter was published as a regular column, complete with by-line. The editor of what was then called the Women's Section asked if I would write a weekly Sunday column about relationships between men and women. *You bet I would!* Not only did I get a by-line, my picture appeared as well! I didn't get paid for the radio or the newspaper. I was beginning to think I was good... for nothing.

What about social life? Put two Key Westers together and they have a party. Put a group together and it's a celebration. What fun that was! There were three excellent community theaters, first-run road shows and an art movie house. Boating, diving, and fishing in the clear, azure waters were a privilege. However, people did not date.

Remember, to travel down that long road meant you really wanted to be in Key West. Or, you were escaping something unpleasant in your life. A death, a divorce, the loss of a career. This was about the time the space program was tightening up. Engineers became dishwashers or waiters. Many of the native Key West men were fishermen or shrimpers, shy around women. Sure, there were lawyers, accountants, small business owners. They all had one thing in common: fear of commitment.

The women were in Key West for the same reasons. They, too, had suffered a loss of some kind. They were strong, feisty and independent. They would never admit they were lonely for the companionship of men.

My radio program and newspaper column had been running for more than a year when I got a nasty flu that prevented me from doing the show or writing the column for a week. Both the paper and the station announced I was ill.

The doorbell rang. By the time I got to the door, there was no one there. But there were flowers and a bowl of soup.

The doorbell rang all day and each time I went to the door, I found flowers, honey, tea bags and enough "invalid food" to supply the entire naval base.

Obviously, the Islanders took care of their own. There were many single people on the Island with no support groups. Why shouldn't we all band together and lend a hand when needed?

I was well enough the following week to write and speak, so I thanked everyone who had come to my rescue; I am not sure what I would have done without their help. I asked single people to help other singles who were ill or needed a friend. It's a small island and everyone knows who's hurting.

There would be nothing formal about this. It would be people doing for people. I asked a very nice hotel if we could have a "get-to-know-each-other dance." Everyone would pay his own tab and there would be no charge for the hall.

Seventy-three people showed up. That was the beginning of the Singles Club. Within two weeks, other hotels offered their premises for "the dances." People started to pair up for theater, movies and walks around the island. We were like teenagers – no commitment – free to date whomever we wanted. Mostly nothing serious, though after awhile there were a few weddings.

How lovely it was to share the island with friends.

The genie was really out of the bottle now.

SANTERIA

Ask anyone in Key West if they believe in Santeria and they'll ask, "What's that?" Give them a minute and they'll come up with some glib remark such as, "It doesn't bother me. I just kick the dead chickens out of the way."

Santeria has played a part in the religious community of Key West since the first slaves arrived. Their incredible stories were told with the integrity of true believers. Members of the island medical and legal professions often see the evidence. Doctors tell of patients who have mortgaged their homes to pay for cures.

Santeria is a religious potpourri of Roman Catholicism, superstition, and Yoruba, the religion of Nigeria where most of the slaves originated. The Oricha (gods) worshipped by the blacks found no favor with the conquerors, who expected their slaves to convert to Catholicism. So when the slaves came to the Americas their gods were given the names of Catholic saints. They erected statues resembling the saints, but the spirits inhabiting those statues were held to be those of the ancient Oricha. The statues in many yards and the beads of different colors around many necks attest to the worship of Oricha in Key West.

According to practitioners, Santeria is not a negative religion. Its devotees say it's as

73

Christian as Catholicism, and indeed predates the Catholic religion. The Catholic Church officially considers it a religion of fear and frowns upon its practice. Psychiatric research in South Florida has found Santeria to be a religion based on cures and optimism. It seeks practical and immediate answers to problems. To believers, it's a kind of mental healing without years on the couch of modern psychiatry.

Santeria offers its practitioners the opportunity to take direct action. They are able to cope in a very direct way with their problems. The appropriate saint sends them out to find certain objects, then tells them what to do. It's a hands-on religion, in which the believer not only prays for help, but then goes out and does what he's told.

Want to give it a try?

- Is there a rival for the affections of your beloved? Take an egg from a black hen, write your rival's name on it, and throw the egg over his house.
- Your new love not passionate? Find a two-tailed lizard, boil it in olive oil, and anoint your lover.
- Ladies, want to make sure your lover remains faithful? Once a month, put one teaspoon of menstrual blood in his morning coffee.
- Men, want to know if your lady is faithful? Put a lodestone under her pillow. If she's

chaste, she'll embrace you. If not, she'll fall out of bed.

- Want someone to confess? Take the tongue from a live frog and put the frog back in the water. Lay the tongue on the heart of the sleeping person. He'll confess in his sleep.
- Do you wake up in the morning with bruises on your body? The spirit of a jealous lover is living inside you. Get a live chicken and toss it over the cemetery gates at midnight. Don't look back.
- Need a job? Put a raw egg in water for seven days. On the seventh day, walk 50 feet and throw the egg to your right. Run... it smells bad.
- Want someone to leave town? Give him a pair of shoes. Want to bug someone? Put nutmeg in his shoes.
- Are you bothered by asthma? Drink a broth made of lizards boiled in milk. Hiccups? Spit on a piece of brown paper; put it on your forehead. Constipation? Wash some earthworms in white wine, dry them and beat into a powder. Add saffron, put it all in home brew. Enjoy.
- Have a bad cut? Get some aloe, dried horse dung, and the blood of a black cat. Make a paste and apply to the wound.
- Do you have stomach pain? (1) Boil onions in water. (2) Have someone knead your back with warm olive oil until you hear a crack. (3) Drink the onion juice.

- Hurricane coming? Put two crossed knives in the yard, or a knife under your mattress, or bake a ham.

Are there many believers in Key West? According to a local Santero, at least one-third of the Cuban community actively participates and the rest tune in when their lives go off key.

Do I believe? Well, I may have taken a couple of precautions when I started this story. Just ignore the upside-down broom at my door, the red candles everywhere, and the water under the bed. So what if there's a little red bag sewn to my bra and garlic in my pocket?

We need all the help we can get.

THE DOLL

I feel chills this sunny morning as I watch a doll wash up on the beach. It has all the characteristics of a Santeria doll: black, with a kerchief tied around her head and a scarf around her neck, a full dress, and an apron, its ties circling her plump body.

She brings to mind another doll that had washed up on shore, its arms tightly bound at its sides. The head was completely turned around, its chest crushed. A gutted dog lay a little way down the beach.

I remember two pigeons, their heads torn from their bodies, part of a macabre scene in front of the judicial chambers of the Key West courthouse. A Ron Rico rum bottle held a white candle. Another doll, this one a GI Joe, had blood on his forehead. His uniform was stained crimson. He stood guard over the spectacle. Drops of blood were scattered across the doorway that led to the Judicial Court.

And now I remember the bizarre things that happened to me.

My experience with Santeria began in May 1982. I was asked to write a piece on the practice of the Afro-Cuban religion in the Florida Keys.

I went to the public library to begin my research, but I found that little had been written about Santeria. I checked out the one book that might have some information and took it home.

'Home' was an old conch house in Old Town, Key West. Behind the house was a private, secluded garden that could not be seen from the street. The only access was through the house. A huge matrimonial hammock, secured with extra thick nautical rope, hung between two coconut palms.

I took the book into the garden, got into the hammock and opened the book – and the hammock crashed to the ground. The ropes were not frayed. They were not cut. There was no logical reason for that hammock to have fallen. I got myself up and examined my sore spots, which would later become bruises of sunset colors and magnitude.

I took the book into the house and sat in a chair. I gritted my teeth, gathered all my brave and picked up the book. I put on my glasses and both lenses popped out.

A few days later, the book and I were at the kitchen table. My new electric coffee pot, also on the table, started to smoke and sputter. There was no damage to the cord or the outlet. It was just smoking. *By now, so was I. What had I gotten myself into?*

On my way to an interview the next day, I had not one but two flat tires. A few days later my hammock was stolen from my virtually inaccessible garden. Nothing else was taken.

Santeria is considered to be "good voodoo," not intended to harm an individual. It is used simply to produce horror. When extreme measures are needed to attain results, some rituals may include the sacrifice of animals and the use of dolls. For instance, if my boyfriend is attracted to you, I will get a voodoo doll. I will tell the gods this doll symbolizes you and I will stick a pin somewhere in your body, wherever I think it will cause the most pain. Does it work? Ask a believer.

Now, five years later, I stand in the bright sunshine, staring down at a doll washed up on the seashore. The tide is coming in and the doll is in danger of being washed away by the next wave. I bend down to pick her up and can't do it. With my toe I nudge her a little further up the beach. A wave tickles her feet; her body rocks with the movement. I lean over again and pick her up by the hand. She is heavy with sand and water. I feel carefully over her small body searching for the pins that might be there. There are none.

I walk up the beach holding the doll. She feels warm and alive. I find myself talking to her, telling her my joys and fears. I walk and talk of good things and bad for a half-hour.

We reach my apartment building. I turn on the pool shower and carefully wash all the sand from her clothes. I open the folds and pleats of her garments and rinse away the broken shells. I wash her face.

She is clean, but I'm afraid to bring her into my apartment. Instead, I take her to the laundry room and set her on a shelf.

"You'll be safe here," I say. "A grandmother will take you home and sit you in the sun and give you to her little granddaughter who will hug you and love you."

I look back for a moment and take the elevator to my apartment. As I put my key in the door, a shiver goes through my entire body. I run down six flights of stairs. This ominous doll is not a toy for a child.

I tear open the laundry room door.

The doll is gone.

THE CANDIDATE

The City

Take the tourists out of Key West and you have a typical small town. Right?

Wrong. You have a community of curmudgeons who came down a long road to get there. No one arrives in Key West by accident. It is a destination city. You also have the indigenous population – the Conchs (Konks). As stubborn a people as you'll ever meet.

When I was approached by the city fathers to run for the position of mayor, hundreds of reason why I shouldn't went through my mind. Too much was happening too fast.

Every week contractors, real estate people, investors appeared in front of The City Commission seeking building variances. The waters surrounding the island were befouled, no longer a spectacular spot for diving.

But one overriding thought persuaded me to say yes. The small fishing village was fading away. The "progress" needed to be sensible and the damage needed to be corrected. Perhaps I could help maintain the balance on the Commission that had held the city together.

The Campaign

The campaign was hard work and long hours. But what fun it was!

There are all kinds of technicalities and legalities involved in running a campaign. You need a chairperson, a treasurer, a lawyer and many committees. Most of all, you need money. Money for television, radio commercials and newspaper ads. You need money for postage and parties. I wondered how I would feel with my hand out. I had never asked for even a penny in my life.

Luckily, I had lots of volunteers. The committees filled up quickly and each one had a capable person at the helm. The lawyer, treasurer and chairperson came to me and asked to work on the campaign. I couldn't say "Yes" fast enough.

We were staffed. Now the speeches started. I spoke to small groups in homes, larger club groups and even in gymnasiums.

We set the date for our first fundraising event. Now it was time to send out invitations.

We had to pay the printer. He was the best in town and all the candidates went to him. He couldn't possibly provide invitations, posters, thank you cards and all the other printed materials, gratis, to every candidate.

I invited the addressing committee to my house. We set up card tables and they merged into their groups – addressing, stuffing, sealing and stamping. I sat at each table and worked with them. Good advice from an old warhorse of a campaigner.

It was finally the night of the fundraiser. It had taken us less than a week to get it together. Just enough time for the invitations to be delivered.

The contribution committee sat at a long banquet table at the entrance. They collected the money and made out the receipts we'd had printed.

The restaurant looked lovely, the food was delicious and the music was perfect.

I gave my speech, thanked everyone for being there and went out on the floor to meet and greet. We had sent out almost 400 invitations and it seemed everyone was there.

As I walked around, I recognized a man from the other camp. I told him I was happy to see him and asked how the other candidate was doing. We shook hands and when our handshake broke I found five hundred dollars in my hand. I thanked him and I sent someone to find the treasurer to record the transaction.

"No, no treasurer," the man told me. "I give every candidate the same amount of money. This is yours."

The man was a building contractor who was doing all he could to get tall hotels in Key West. I gave the money back to him and told him I would not take any contribution that could not be recorded. I thanked him and he stormed out.

The party was a success. We raised enough money for the whole campaign and did not need another fundraiser.

I liked campaigning. People really listen to what you say. They misquote you later, but that's okay. You can always straighten it out.

The campaign period in Key West is short – only a month or so. It was great fun and I loved it.

I lost.

WITH EGRETS:
Florida, 50 Years Ago

The road gleamed with at least fifty egrets daintily showering themselves in the roadside lagoon. Their white feathers glistened, their yellow beaks were the color of sunshine and their legs, with backward knees, somehow kept them upright.

It had been at least fifty years since I last saw a flock of egrets. Or a flock of any birds.

Polluted air and water fouled their homes. Automobiles have dramatically lessened their numbers. The flocks are gone.

Another hot day in sub-tropical Florida. The birds – a vision, perhaps? No, they had to be real.

A rush of glee brightened my whole body. They're coming back! The birds are coming back!

The birds at the side of the road brought home glorious memories of an enchanted Florida, forty years ago.

The Atlantic Ocean and the Gulf of Mexico surround the island of Key West. Back in the sixties, the waters were full of sea life. Being tickled by schools of tropical fish while snorkeling was a benefit Key West offered back then.

Those watery schools were crowded. Hundreds, perhaps thousands, of fish traveled together. To go around them was not practical. So we swam through them, the fish tickling our bodies as they skimmed over us. It's hard to laugh with a snorkel in your mouth. We were the strangers here. We were swimming in their waters.

There was no reason to hire a boat and captain to explore the reefs. A short swim would deliver us to the pristine coral rocks teeming with small fish, turtles, crabs and myriad other sea creatures. The sun's rays cut through the water, turning the reef a glistening white aglow with subtle pink highlights.

Schools of grouper and snapper swam along with us.

A huge sea turtle, out for his daily exercise, crawled along next to me for a moment. I was too fast for him and outdistanced him in a deliberate doggie paddle.

Gay, my snorkeling buddy, knew the dock off U.S. A1A was the best snorkeling area in Key West. It was also the daytime gathering place for the gay population of Key West. The pier was called Dick Dock.

Gay was visually impaired. Her eyeglass prescription was ground into the clear portion of her mask. I took it upon myself to know where Gay was in the water at all times. One day, I looked around and could not see her.

Maybe she swam up to the surface, I thought. Quickly I made my way to the sunshine. I still could not see her. There, in the shadow of

Dick Dock, I shouted "Gay! Gay! Where are you, Gay?" I could not imagine why everyone on the dock hurried to the north side of the pier to see who was shouting.

And Gay? There she was, strolling down the beach, her flippers dangling from her hand. Seems she couldn't get my attention below and really had to go use the facilities. A fine snorkeling buddy I turned out to be.

Today the reefs are far from shore, and you need to motor out many miles. Snorkelers, with only their snorkels, masks and fins, are wary of venturing out into the deep water. So the remaining reefs are left to those who attend Scuba classes and earn their certificates.

Memories are not enough. I want the birds and the waters to live the way they did fifty years ago. I want to swim again in waters that are home to millions of brightly colored tropical fish and all their brothers and sisters, nieces and nephews and other marine relatives. I want flocks of birds to poop on our cars and eat the bugs.

It's another hot day in sub-tropical Florida. The gathering of egrets at the side of the road ... a hopeful harbinger announcing things to come? Or just a long ago memory?

THE TOUR DIRECTOR

Part One

It was my fourth trip to the Soviet Union in as many months. It was cold, very cold, and I had forgotten to bring my boots. But I was doing exactly what I wanted to do: TRAVEL with a capital T.

My friend and I started a travel company to scratch that travel itch. That's not how it worked. *Shoestring Adventures* was a successful venture. We stayed home while other people went off on the exciting trips we planned for them.

I interviewed with several of the top tour companies and was hired by all of them. I was now a freelance Tour Director who actually traveled. My special areas were the old Soviet Union, Alaska and South America. No, I do not speak Russian or Spanish. I needed an interpreter 24 hours a day, seven days a week. You'd be amazed at the number of middle-of-the-night emergency trips we made to hospitals.

This trip started, as most of the Russian trips do, at JFK airport in New York. The 39 people on the tour flew into Kennedy from all parts of the United States and Canada. I picked them up at designated meeting points in Kennedy's International Terminal. When we were all together, I told them what to expect at Soviet

Immigration and Customs and urged them to get some rest on the plane. We were in for a busy ten days: three days in Moscow, three in St. Petersburg, two in Tbilisi, and two travel days.

The flight was on time. We boarded and everyone settled in. The seat belt sign went out and I got up. This was the only chance I had to spend personal time with each individual and to answer questions ... many questions. Like, "How long are we allowed to sleep on the plane?" And my favorite, "I think I left my passport on the counter in Miami. Will they ask for it in Moscow?"

After an uneventful flight, we landed at Moscow Airport and got through the dreaded Immigration and Customs without any problems. We met Irena, the interpreter for this trip. Her English was excellent but she was resentful of my job. I knew in the first five minutes, she felt she could do the whole thing without everything flowing through me. She was probably right.

We boarded our very comfortable Mercedes coach and cruised to our hotel. Hotels on these tours are huge. They're four-star establishments, not as luxurious as American hotels but comfortable, with good security.

We had a light lunch in the dining room and went to our rooms. I left reminder calls for every room to meet at 7:30 for dinner. I called Irena and invited her to my room for tea. I wanted to mend fences before they were broken. She said "nyet." Okay, then. I could take a nap.

The next two days were full. The tour members were having a sensational time. It was cold but everyone had brought warm clothes. I really missed my boots.

On the third night, we went to the Moscow Circus. The sidewalks were slippery and I fell, landing on my arm. *Darn those forgotten boots.* "I'm fine, I'm really fine. Go find your seats. It's a wonderful circus. We'll meet right here afterward."

I found Irena during intermission. "Irena, I've broken my arm. I've done it before and I recognize the feeling. We'll have to go to the hospital when everyone is settled in their rooms."

"It is not broken. You just want attention. I will not go with you to hospital," said my Russian good will ambassador.

Here I am in Moscow, Russia, responsible for 39 people who deserve my attention. I have a bus driver who understands no English. The interpreter is recalcitrant and resentful. And I have a broken arm. The Tour Director manual didn't cover this.

Part Two

We're still at the Moscow Circus and the show should be over in a half-hour. We'll get back to the hotel and once everyone is settled in, I'll get a cab and go to the hospital by myself. For heaven's sake, I can do it.

The lights go up and I go to our group's meeting place. Everyone is smiling and laughing and talking about the clowns. They ask how my arm is. I'm eager for us to get on the coach and head back to the hotel.

Here comes Irena, the interpreter. "Masha," she yells from the arena door. "Let's take our friends on a night coach tour of Moscow."

A night tour of Moscow? Give me a break. Moscow is a dismal city after dark. It's not like New York or Paris or even London. If I say no, the travelers will think they're missing something. If I say yes, there is nothing to see and they will be disappointed. My arm aches. I know it's broken; there's that same burning sensation I had last time.

"All right, Irena," I shout back to her. "We'll see if the lights are on tonight. You know, sometimes they are not lit. Tell the driver where to go."

I'd like to tell Irena where to go.

We drive around aimlessly for a time, while I tell the group what we're doing tomorrow. I remind them there is a 6:30 wake-up call. We're taking an early train to St. Petersburg, which takes only five hours. The later trains take up to ten hours. And the highway is two lanes except for a few small stretches, so forget the coach.

It's almost midnight when we pull up to the hotel, thanks to Irena's night tour. I'm too tired to start looking for hospitals now. I'll take a sleeping pill and some Tylenol and hope for a decent night's sleep.

There is no time for hospitals in the morning. Luckily, I travel with many large, color-coordinated silk scarves. I fashion a sling for my arm and feel a tad more comfortable.

I'll have my arm looked at in St. Petersburg, although the schedule is daunting. We have two days to go through the Hermitage, see Peter the Great's Castle and Catherine's Palace. We'll take a short walking tour, have a vodka-and-food tasting in a café, and attend the Kirov Ballet. We fly out of St. Petersburg the second night for Tbilisi.

Early on our first morning in St. Petersburg, I manage to get to a doctor's office near the hotel. They explain, through mime, that they only treat the center of the body, not arms or legs. The next morning, I take a cab to the closest hospital. No interpreter. I try to explain, through gestures, that I want an X-ray and a cast. No luck.

We fly into Tbilisi that night.

The next day is a sleep-late morning. I am able to get to the hospital. No one speaks English. Finally, someone remembers there is a bi-lingual American patient in the hospital.

By now, there's quite a crowd of us and we all go to his room. He makes the medical team understand that I want an X-ray and a cast for my arm if it is broken. "Ah, da," was heard in the room.

Then I said I wanted to take the X-ray to my doctor in the United States. "Nyet, Russia's medical program is run by the State and the X-ray belongs to the government." But, they'll give me a note in Latin, the universal language of medicine, for my doctor.

My arm *is* broken. The nurse dunks some limp, dirty gauze into plaster and the doctor wraps my arm. I can turn my arm in the cast.

I get home and hug my doctor with one arm. He says, "What have you done this time, Marsha?"

ON THE WAY TO ANTARCTICA

Two hours in the car, ten hours on a plane and five days at sea. Was it worth it? You bet your sweet bippy it was. My daughter, her husband and I were on our way to Antarctica, a place few people will ever see ... not even in their wildest dreams.

We flew from Miami to Buenos Aires, the cruise departure port. After three days in Buenos Aires, we departed for the Antarctic. The seas were calm, with hardly any wind. The temperature was 83 degrees.

Four days later, we arrived at Stanley, capital of the Falkland Islands. We were not yet in Antarctica but the weather was sure changing. The winds blew at 27 mph and the temperature was 48 degrees.

The Falklands are best remembered for the 1982 territorial, oil war between England and Argentina. Before we disembarked, we were warned not to wear clothing with Argentinean logos. The political stance of each country is still unfriendly. Large areas of Stanley are cordoned off, posted with signs warning of landmines and unexploded ordinance.

We saw our first penguins in the Falklands, some of them right there in the danger zones.

These birds don't weigh enough to set off the mines left over from the war.

Recent movies have featured the large Emperor and King penguins. We saw the smaller Adelies and Rockhoppers.

There were more than two hundred Adelies on the beach in their small social groups. They were exactly as I had pictured, clad in their formal finery. Adelies stand about 30 inches tall and weigh up to eleven pounds. Population: approximately 2.5 million pair in the Antarctic region.

Penquins do not fly but are fast swimmers, some up to 40 mph. Their stubby wings help them glide through the water. Truly flightless, penguins spend as much as 75 percent of their lives at sea. On the beach, they toddle around on their short legs.

Penguins are noisy! Each type has a different call. Some cackle like hens, some trumpet and some bray like donkeys. Parents and chicks recognize each other's voices.

Penguins breed in large colonies, with as many as 180,000 birds. Each pair incubates one or two eggs, taking turns sitting on them. While one sits, the other searches for food. Once hatched, the chicks are fed by mom or dad. Food is digested by the parent and then regurgitated into the chick's mouth. It works.

Penguins are fascinating oddball birds, elegant, funny and hardy. I was enchanted. I could have watched them for hours, but sadly, it was time for lunch.

We ordered freshly caught fish and chips. I wanted mine in a newspaper cone. But no, even at the end of the world, newspaper cones are against health laws. I was grouchy, but the fish was good.

We strolled the streets of Stanley. The natives smiled and said, "How do?" We saw a lawyer's office, an accountant's, a small grocery and a garage. The other shops were tourist oriented. I hope that works for the town. We'd been told our ship might be the last cruise ship permitted to sail the Antarctic Peninsula. Eco-friendly changes are being considered for the Antarctic Charter.

The Antarctic has no indigenous inhabitants, but there are permanent and summer-only staffed research stations. The longest stay of any researcher has been 2 ½ years. The population varies from 1,000 in winter to 4,000 in summer.

We headed back to the ship after a few pleasant hours in Stanley. Up and down in a small boat, fighting 13-foot waves. I can't remember if the butt hits the bench on an up or down wave. I know we slapped the bench on one or the other; probably even both cheeks at the same time.

It is now about 2:00 in the afternoon. We have the rest of today and all of tomorrow before we are actually in the Antarctic. We will attend lectures on the ship about this lonely continent.

I can hardly wait to get there ...

Changing Parts

Changing parts will not make a Rolls Royce out of a Ford.

The Prosthesis
The Sum of My Parts
Plus-Size Women
My Chinny-Chin-Chin

THE PROSTHESIS

For eleven years, I've been wearing my prosthesis wrong side up. I have been walking around for more than a decade with an upside-down boob ... and no one ever said a word.

Post-mastectomy bras have pockets on the inside of the cup. These pockets are shaped like the prosthesis (also called a *realistic breast form*). All these years, I've paid no attention and just shoved the form into the pocket. It took some maneuvering to do it wrong. I finally figured it out a couple of weeks ago. Duh!

There have been many improvements in both softwear and hardwear in eleven years. The prosthesis is lighter and cooler and generally easier to wear ... if you wear it right side up.

Fittings are thorough and complete. First, you need a new bra. Let's talk about the bra fitter. She looks like a PLAYBOY centerfold, except she does not have a crease down the middle. Is there no justice?

The bra fitter brings two bras into the fitting room, fully aware she'll need to show at least a dozen more. Some bras get tried on three and four times. Some bras are dismissed with a wave of the hand. I always ask my daughter to come to fittings. She, the fitter and I all have to decide on one bra. When everyone finally agrees one bra is better than all the others, it's time to choose the prosthesis.

Surprisingly, that's easier than selecting the bra. My criteria are simple:
- ✓ It must be flexible, with realistic movement.
- ✓ It must have a flat back to contour to the chest wall.
- ✓ It must not shift or slide.
- ✓ It must be safe in chlorine and salt water.

I have recently added one more criterion for the prosthesis:
- ✓ It must have an arrow.

THE SUM OF MY PARTS

Years ago, a joke made the rounds. It was about a young couple on their honeymoon. The bride took off her wig and put it in the drawer. She had four false teeth. She took them out and put them in the drawer. She then removed two falsies and put them in the drawer. Having removed her wig, her teeth and both her boobs, she asked, "Honey, are you coming to bed?"

"No way," he replied. "I'm sleeping in the drawer."

There is not much I can put in a drawer. Most of my new parts are attached to me in some way. Let's start at the top.

In my head are several staples following a brain aneurysm. I have a magnetic paper clip holder on my desk. At times, I picture the staples spinning around in my brain due to the magnetic field.

I have dental implants, which are definitely not supposed to come out. I don't trust much anymore. I was at dinner on a cruise ship, took a bite of a roll and there was my tooth. There was also a huge gap right in the middle of my upper teeth. I didn't smile much that trip.

I never noticed I kept my hand on my right bum all the time, particularly going up stairs, until a friend pointed it out to me. It was then I realized I was in pain. The doctor said "hip replacement." When my left hand found my left bum, I went back to the doctor and told him I needed another hip. I now have two new hips and a new knee. I wonder what the replacements cost without all the physicians' fees and hospital expenses.

The cost of a body's minerals, calcium, skin and all that stuff is $4.50. The skin is the most expensive, about $2.50. My body is missing some bones, so I figure my basic cost is about $3.75.

Finally we get to the interesting part. My prostheses are titanium. A two-gram bar sells for $76. A titanium wedding ring costs $195. I figure a wedding ring weighs a half-ounce. Titanium is very light so it's probably less, but I'll go with the half-ounce. I think each of the three prostheses weighs at least 30% more than the ring. So, we need to convert ounces into grams or grams into ounces. In either case, it boggles my mind.

If anyone can calculate the sum of all my parts, I would be grateful. In the meantime, my hairbrush has more hair in it than it used to and my dental implants are feeling wobbly. Guess I'd better empty a drawer.

PLUS-SIZE WOMEN

She weighs 230 pounds but there is something sensuous about her. Those 230 pounds glide over her 5'7'' frame. Her body is firm. Nothing jiggles. Nothing looks out of place. Her ideal weight is between 146 and 167 pounds. She is overweight, but not obese. She exercises and walks each day.

Cassie is a plus-size runway model who gets more calls for photo jobs every day. Why is Cassie one of the most popular models in the business? Because one-third of the population of the United States is overweight. Another one-third is obese, defined as 100 or more pounds over ideal weight. These are adults, teenagers and children.

There is no way to sugarcoat this: 2/3 of our population is overweight.

Obesity is quickly pushing tobacco out of first place in causing serious illnesses and early fatalities. According to the U.S. Surgeon General, obesity is responsible for 300,000 deaths a year in the United States. Being obese is reaching epidemic proportions in North America.

One of the initial concerns is how you feel about yourself. In a 2012 interview, Queen Latifah suggested five ways to increase self-esteem for overweight women.

1. Don't feast your eyes on models, no matter how thin or overweight the model is. The

more models they see, overweight women say, the worse they feel about themselves.

2. <u>Move your body</u>. Put your body through the paces. Do whatever you love to do: dance, swim, hike, yoga. Don't fall into the "how I look" trap. "I'm too fat. I'll look stupid in yoga class." Check out the 10 Minute Solutions DVDs. Move your body and get your blood boiling at least three times a week.

3. <u>Know your self-esteem pitfalls.</u> Figure out when you feel the worst about yourself. Is it after a visit or phone call with your mom or sister? Is it at work when a certain coworker is around? Is it at night when you're tired and stressed? Simply being aware that you will feel bad about yourself after X happens will help you avoid the consequences. My consequence is binge eating.

4. <u>Differentiate between external and internal triggers.</u> An example of an external trigger: when someone criticizes or insults you. An internal trigger: when you tell yourself you're overweight because you're bad, worthless, dumb or lazy. Can you do anything about the trigger that decreases your self-esteem most often? Sure you can. Taking control of situations and people that harm your self-esteem is empowering. Anything that empowers you will increase

your self-esteem. Which will take off some pounds.

5. <u>Keep doing what you're good at</u>. Identifying your best qualities is difficult for many women. Not all of us have been taught to be our own cheerleaders. We tend to focus on our weaknesses and mistakes, not on the things we do well. To increase your self-esteem, remember what you are good at ... and do it regularly.

Savor your ability and talent. It sets you apart and makes you special. Oddly enough, you will begin to lose weight.

MY CHINNY-CHIN-CHIN

In 1979 I had my hysterectomy. My husband and I had been legally separated for several years and we had just started negotiating our divorce. The hospital refused my doctor the use of an operating room until my soon-to-be ex-husband gave his permission for a hysterectomy.

He said, "No way."

I could feel my blood boil. It was none of his business. At 45, I was certainly an adult, was mentally stable, and had made no outrageous decisions about the children's lives or my own.

This was the era of Women's Lib. The Establishment was at the peak of its crusade for keeping women in their place. And the hospital was very much a part of that Establishment.

I called my attorney to get started on planning our strategy.

He presented a tight, logical case to the court. Finally I was able to make my own decisions about my body. The whole project took six months – a long time since the surgery was medically necessary.

The operation was a success except for one small matter. They discovered my body was not producing testosterone. Did you even know women had testosterone in their makeup? Men have female hormones so we're even. I was given a couple of testosterone injections and was feeling feisty again. All was well. I was discharged from the hospital and had an easy recovery.

A couple of months later, I noticed a little more hair on my upper lip. My eyebrows were shaggier. Trips to the beauty salon for waxing became more frequent.

Then, one day, there were bristles on my chin. The next day I had a little beard. I am convinced this was the result of those testosterone injections. No doctor, no lab, no 'expert' will ever prove otherwise.

I was able to maintain the upper lip and eyebrows with twice-a-month visits to the beauty salon. But the chin was serious. It needed almost daily care. I did the worst thing possible; I started shaving my chin. Once in the morning seemed to do the job – until 5:00 o'clock shadow crept in. I was now shaving twice a day.

This went on for years. I became an expert on different types of razors. Electric didn't do the job. I couldn't bring myself to throw away disposable razors after only one use. As a result, I kept them on the job until they were as dull as window scrapers.

Oil of Olay was selling a new razor with a feminine shaving cream built into the razor's edge. Forget it. The cream didn't release, and the razor became dull. I never did find a decent razor.

Time passed. As I got older my hands started to shake and my vision diminished. I could no longer shave safely, and my twice-monthly visit to the waxer would not work for the chin. Waxing the stubble didn't do it. The whiskers had to be long enough for the wax to grab onto them. Otherwise, the pull of the wax removed the hair only at skin level. Not much help.

So the hair grows long and I am embarrassed to be among people. I need to visit the beauty shop every seven to ten days.

It seems my life and wallet revolve around the hair on my chinny-chin-chin.

Changing Seasons

Deep in December, it's hard to remember...
(with apologies to The Fantasticks)

Harry
Growing Old Sucks
The Great Gift Dilemma
Happy Birthday to Me
Tax Time
Memorial Day
Misdial Is Not a Word
Sunrise, Sunset

HARRY

Harry was almost perfect and I loved him so much. So what if he couldn't see too well and didn't hear everything I said. He never asked for help and managed almost everything on his own.

We went for long walks and afterwards we curled up in bed for a nap.

I guess there *was* one thing about Harry. He preferred to eat alone. Oh well, I could deal with that. I would serve his food in his favorite place on the balcony and I would eat, by myself, at the table. That was okay with me.

We snuggled while watching television and he sat next to me as I read the daily newspaper aloud.

Then Harry became ill. He was listless, couldn't keep food down and ran a high temperature. His heart raced and he could hardly lift his head.

We went to the doctor. He said Harry was fading quickly and there was nothing he could do.

I held Harry in my arms as life left his little body.

We buried Harry under a tree in the back yard. I found a small doggie toy and placed it on his grave.

What a brave little Yorkie was Harry.

GROWING OLD SUCKS
(SOMETIMES)

Forget the aches and pains. Forget the almost-daily doctors' visits. And forget the pills... the pills you take on a twice-daily schedule.

There are worse things coming.

This was the week I came to the realization I could not help solve my children's problems, nor did they ask for my help. For the first time, I felt old and useless. My children hired two attorneys, each a specialist in their field of law, at a combined cost of a thousand dollars an hour. Most days run about six hours. The case involves intellectual property rights, internet websites, trademarks, plagiarism and anything else you can imagine. Or maybe you can't.

How can I have the audacity to think I can solve, or even oversee, the management of such a problem?

So, I become depressed, on many levels. I worry about the injustice and the anguish the children are going through. I also realize that I am getting older. That I am not needed as I was. That I am not as 'sharp' as I was. My son-in-law will be 54 next month and my daughter will be 50 on her next birthday. For heaven's sake, why can't I respect that?

I try to hide my feelings, but somehow my daughter always knows. Even with all the havoc in her life, she keeps asking, "What's wrong, Mom?" I finally tell her and tears come to her eyes. Now I am back in the loop and copied on everything.

If I want to change a line in a document, I tell them. If the change is accepted, that's okay. If not, that's okay, too.

I have discovered there is old wisdom and young wisdom. I have discovered that children grow up. They become adults and need to be respected and treated as such.

I have also discovered it's not how old you are. It's how much love there is.

THE GREAT GIFT DILEMMA

July. Record-breaking heat and drought. Hot and dry as a camel's tongue. And another thing to add to the fire: Christmas-in-July sales. Who can even think of Christmas when it's 100 degrees in Minneapolis?

Don't sweat it. I spoke with Carol Hemingway, noted astrologer and lecturer, about gift giving. Evidently, there is consolation in the constellations. Hemingway has come up with a gift list according to astrological signs.

Aries

Always in the midst of an exciting adventure, the Aries would like a squad car complete with flashing red lights or a one-way ticket on a fire engine. A "novelty" gift would be fun. How about a car license plate that says "Leader?"

Taurus

Powerful Taurus is bent on amassing a great fortune. A three-month CD (certificate of deposit) opened with a thousand dollars, designer clothes and beautiful things (read expensive) are all gift well received by Taureans.

Gemini

Because they are always in a hurry, Geminis would appreciate a microwave oven. No cigarettes! – They traditionally have bad lungs.

119

Anything to do with communication and/or a ticket on the fastest transportation available. They like variety so don't give a tie every year. They love to talk so a smartphone would be perfect.

Cancer

Poor Cancer, always off balance. More than unsettled, he is often unstable. Buy something for the home, a frivolous thing. Give a two-week vacation in a log cabin or a Family Tree History. Most of all, give LOVE.

Leo

The essence of light and comprehension. Clears the air, provides guidance and restores harmony. Also wants to be leader of the pack. Give your Leo a small country to run or a spotlight with a year's supply of bulbs.

Virgo

The practicality of Virgo finds the theories of Leo definitely too confusing. Exasperation sets in. Buy Virgos their own hospital or clinic to administer. Whatever you buy, make certain it is not on sale or an imperfect second. A gift certificate to an analyst is good; the Virgo will analyze the analyst. You may give a diet book but no artificial food. A dictionary to carry is always good for a Virgo.

Libra

The easy-going Libra announces that leisure is the goal of life. Find your Libra a mate and a marriage license. Anything mentally stimulating: like a psychology book, preferably on relationships.

Scorpio

Scorpio gets things back on track after a month of Libra's lackadaisical lifestyle. The Scorpio sets hidden agendas to achieve his idea of life. Nothing superficial for the Scorpio; buy him his own lie detector.

Sagittarius

Scorpio's introspection lasts just a month. Then the expansive Sag takes the upper hand. He announces his notions on the ideal state of things. Books on law, philosophy and religion, a trip to foreign parts, Las Vegas or Atlantic City are good gifts.

Capricorn

Luckily, Capricorn comes along and the period is dominated by the prudence and persistence of this methodical sign. Set up a bank for a Capricorn, complete with vault. Gifts must be sensible; a bag of paper money, for instance.

Aquarius

Aquarius makes certain Capricorn's system does not crumble. Make a contribution to "Defenders of Wildlife" in his name. Any Aquarian wants his own laboratory. Give him anything intellectual.

Pisces

Pisces is the most metaphysically oriented of all the symbols. Pisces love to cry so give them something to cry about. Nothing material – clouds, dreams, poetry books, a piece of sculpture.

This heat wave is going to last for a while. Get in your air-conditioned car and head to the air-conditioned stores.

Just follow the signs.

HAPPY BIRTHDAY TO ME

I recently celebrated my 77th birthday and it got me thinking about why I keep on having them. I have lived longer than any of my family.

My father was 24 when he died; my mother was 22. Both had cancer. My maternal grandparents, aunts and uncles were all in their 50s.

All these early passings had an effect on me when I was raising my own children. I needed them to be as independent as feral cats. I certainly did not think I would be around for them.

The children were encouraged to fend for themselves. Their favorite breakfast was herring and ice cream and that was okay with me. After all, they were getting two of the major food groups.

When Gary was six and Carey was four, they decided to visit Aunt Anne in New York. We lived in Miami. They called for a cab to take them to the airport, which is where we finally found them. I was delighted they had packed a change of underwear.

My children grew to be independent adults.

In my 60s, I was told I had breast cancer and must have surgery the next day. My comment? "Well, it's about time!"

The operation was successful and I opted not to have chemotherapy. Why no chemo?

I asked the doctor if he could guarantee I would remain cancer-free. "No, it could come back", said the doctor. I then asked if the cancer would recur if I did not have treatment. He could not say yes or no. "There are no answers to these questions," said the doctor, shaking his head. The odds were even. After all these years, I was not messing with the odds. This was over eleven years ago and I am still having birthdays.

In my earlier days, I was ready to go to the Great Beyond anytime. Now I find myself making deals for more birthdays.

I will exercise.

I will take a walk each day.

I just want to see my children maintain their independence in their senior years. I want to see my grandchildren grown up. I want to see my great-grandchildren get started in their lives.

I will take the stairs instead of the elevator.

I will not eat so much ice cream.

How about if I work for world peace?

Please, God, let me have more birthdays.

TAX TIME

Well, I had nothing for my writing group this week. Friday just got here too quickly. Too many deadlines. Add income taxes to the mix and we have a formula for disaster. It's my fault, really. Every year I wait until the last possible moment to get it all together.

There is a drawer in my home especially reserved for tax facts, receipts, and validation. Throughout the year, all financial paperwork is literally stuffed into that drawer. Come January 1, the drawer is emptied and everything is jammed into a huge orange tote bag. The bag is set aside until tax time, and the drawer is ready to accept the new year's tax related papers.

Around the end of March, I start getting edgy. I need to organize the tax bag. Maybe I'll even be early this year.

It has never happened.

The contents of the orange bag are now strewn over my bed. I get rubber bands, a stapler and some paper clips. All of this paper has been stuffed into a drawer, then in a bag for a year. It has exploded to fill the surface of my queen-sized bed, a pile two feet high. Now comes the collating of like materials in chronological order. All the credit card statements are rubber-banded together. Bank statements, ditto. And so it goes, until the organizing task is complete.

Ready for the listings? Columns are set up: medical, prescriptions, charitable contributions. If you run a business, such as writing from your home, there are more columns: percentage of utilities, phone, mortgage or rent. Office supplies, postage, occasional office help for one thing or another. As many column headings as you can think of.

We are now ready to put each rubber-banded package in chronological order. First we staple together pages that refer to each other. We then need to extract pertinent information and list it in the appropriate column, highlighting the source as we go along for future reference.

Finally, on April 11 or 12, everything is crammed neatly into a cardboard box and taken to the tax accountant. Another tax year under my belt!

MEMORIAL DAY

My neighbor's door opens and I hear her friend leaving. "Happy Memorial Day," she calls.

"You, too," answers my neighbor.

This year, more than ever, that seems to be the usual salutation for this somber day. Memorial Day is not a "happy day." It is a day of introspection, appreciation and gratitude. Gratitude to the military men and women who lost their lives or limbs in defense of peace, democracy and our country.

The families and veterans who visit the military graves at Arlington Cemetery and in other military cemeteries around the country are not happy. They are proud of their sons, daughters, fathers, mothers, husbands, wives, sisters and brothers. But they are also grieving.

Perhaps the saddest area at Arlington is the Tomb of the Unknown Soldier, which represents the military dead who could not be identified. The Tomb has many visitors. They may be doing homage to a relative, friend or neighbor. No one knows.

After the Civil War, small-town cemeteries for veterans ran out of space. We needed a national cemetery. The government appropriated a site above the Potomac River and Arlington Cemetery was established.

Decoration Day was initiated in many cities, towns and villages, usually in the month of May. Military graves were decorated with wreaths of flowers.

Decoration Day was a solemn occasion created to honor those who died in the service of the U.S. military. It became an official Federal holiday in 1971, to be recognized on the last Monday in May. The name was changed to Memorial Day to emphasize the sober meaning of the day. Picnics, parades and prayer were the traditional tributes of Memorial Days past.

Today

The VFW, cities, and towns still present parades and acknowledgements.

Where are the people? Perhaps watching the war movies on every television channel. Or shopping the Biggest Sales of the Year. Just check your daily newspaper and TV listings.

Sales? Happy Memorial Day?

Bah, humbug.

Rest in peace, brave warriors.

MISDIAL IS NOT A WORD

Are my eyes growing weary? Are my fingers becoming clumsy? Each day I dial more wrong numbers. In the past, when I reached an incorrect answering service, I'd hang up. Now, I leave a message. "Sorry, I've misdialed." I don't get those angry calls any more. "Who are you? Why are you calling my number?"

Last week I made two calls that resulted in memorable misdials.

Call number one:

"Hello. This is the Free Sex Club. If you are a man, press...."

That's when I hung up. There will probably be a nine dollar charge on my phone bill.

Reading this over, I wasn't sure how to spell misdial, with one 's' or two? I looked in the dictionary and discovered that misdial is not a word. It will be before this generation gets much older. What word can I use? How about 'miscall: to call by the wrong name?' Okay, new definition: 'miscall: to call by the wrong number.' I'll call Webster.

There are two-and-a-half pages of 'mis' words in my dictionary. I went down the columns:

- A misanthrope is a people hater. Misogyny is the hatred of marriage. Misogamy is the hatred of women.

- A misdeed is an immoral deed. Misdemeanor, a minor offense. Misdoing is a wrongful act. A miscreant is a villain.
- A mismatch is an unsuitable match. A mish mash is a hodge-podge.
- A miser is a hoarder of wealth. To be miserable is to be wretched, deplorable, despicable.
- A missal is a book of prayers. Missal falls into the 'mis' category by its spelling, not its definition.
- If I'm not mistaken, we're often miscast for perfectly logical reasons.

What was that? What did you say? Oh, call number two? Here it is:

I wanted to return something I'd bought and needed to know if I'd gone beyond the allotted number of days. The phone was answered in the sing-song gibberish of the day.

"Good morning. This is Rxwl Sklf. How may I direct your call?"

"I'd like to talk with the return department, please."

"What department did you say?"

"The return department."

"Madam, this is a rest home. We have no return department."

There was a short pause, filled with silence. Then we both started laughing at the same time.

Obviously, another miscall. I'd better get on that call to Webster.

SUNRISE, SUNSET

When I moved into my home last November, I was astonished that I could see the beginning and end of each day. I would check the times in the newspaper, set my morning alarm for sunrise and make no appointments in the evening, for fear I would miss sunset. Occasionally, I invited close friends to enjoy the sky's magic times with me.

What delightful bookends to my day.

This enchantment lasted for several weeks with small increments of movement. The world was turning. Eventually the world turned away from my sunrise and sunset. I was disconsolate and unsatisfied. My days did not start and they were unfinished.

My life felt the same way. Chores were not completed, books were not read. My patience was waning. My dog spent most of his life in 'time-out.'

My balcony overlooks the river. I found I could see the river tides on the pier supports. Stability began to come back into my life. I began to check the tide times in the newspaper.

I realize that no matter how quirky my life becomes or how the world changes, Mother Nature will keep me in balance. The sun will rise and set on time, no matter where I am. So will the moon. The tide lines on the pier pilings will come at the correct moment, four times a day. What a comfort.

I looked out my window this morning and sunrise was just around the corner. Just another couple of weeks until *my* sun will again rise and set for me.

I smiled. The world is still turning.

Changing Loyalties

*Country and family are two sorts of loyalty.
We don't need any more.*

Long May She Wave
Long Beach
An Overnight Stay
Before and After

LONG MAY SHE WAVE

GeeGee was a handsome man, straight and tall. His steel grey hair had a slight wave and was always neatly combed. GeeGee and Bubby, my grandparents, escaped the pogroms in Russia. They never spoke of those days. My grandfather was an American now and proud of it.

Back in the late '40s and the early '50s, the American flag flew proudly from flagpoles in front of houses and businesses. GeeGee would awaken before dawn on the 14 official flag display days. He knew flag etiquette: flag up at dawn and down at dusk. He knew how to fold it properly. But GeeGee also had a puckish sense of humor. Some years he'd run up the flag on Chanukah, Christmas and Valentine's Day.

My thoughts now travel back more than 69 years. Back to the most patriotic years of our country. Back to the war that was going to end all wars.

Sunday morning, December 7, 1941. I was seven years old, sitting cross-legged on the floor in Tante Molly's living room. Bubby, GeeGee, Tante Molly, her new husband and I were listening to the radio. I remember I was wearing a kilt skirt with a big gold safety pin and my hair was in pigtails. A news bulletin interrupted the program and told the world the United States Navy had been attacked. There were sobs and muffled prayers in the room; bodies swayed back and forth. I didn't understand why the adults were so upset about boats in Hawaii. Heck, I did not even know where Hawaii was. I also did not know what the word "war" really meant. I did not know that Bubby, GeeGee, and Tante Molly had escaped from persecution in Russia and Poland. If "war" was making *them* so upset, what would happen to *me*?

The United States went to war.

Europe had been at war since 1935. People were killed by bombs striking their homes night and day. Survivors lived in shelters. Food was limited. Petrol, as they called gas, was scarce. We heard of the bravery, both civilian and military.

Gas rationing was initiated in the United States in 1942. Ration decals were pasted on car windshields:

Class A cars received the least amount because usage was nonessential.

Class B cars belonged to people who needed to drive for work.

Class C cars usually belonged to doctors and law enforcement drivers.

Class X was quickly cancelled after much finger pointing. This class was for "very important" people, such as Senators and members of the House of Representatives.

The Office of Price Administration (OPA) issued food ration books in April of 1942. Each member of the household received a book. Coffee stamps were removed from books issued to children under 15. Red stamps were for meat and meat products: butter, fats, cheese, canned milk and canned fish. A shopper could earn two extra red points for every pound of meat fat turned in to the local butcher. Poultry was not rationed. Green, brown or blue stamps were for canned vegetables, juices, baby food and dried fruit.

Neighborhood Victory Gardens bloomed everywhere. They brightened the landscapes of cities and small towns. The vibrant reds of the tomatoes, red peppers and strawberries highlighted the subtle greens of peppers and broccoli. White cauliflower and the gentle green of celery completed the bouquet. Over to the side were onions, sweet and white potatoes and carrots.

Young men were drafted into the armed services and thousands volunteered. White flags with red borders appeared in windows; a gold star centered on the white background meant a soldier had died in defense of his country. Our flag had a blue star, which meant our soldier was in active service.

Our soldier was my Uncle Mitt. He was an athletic kind of guy. Not too tall but in great physical shape. Despite his short stature he was the star of his high school basketball team. Uncle Mitt loved clothes and when he graduated from school, he went to work in a haberdashery store. Uncle Mitt enlisted in the Air Force and he and Aunt Ruthie got married before he was sent to Europe. Aunt Ruthie wore traditional white and

Uncle Mitt proudly wore the khaki uniform of an Air Force NCO instead of one of his natty suits.

His assignment: tail gunner on a B-17, the Flying Fortress. The Brits bombed their targets during the night. The Yanks attacked during the more vulnerable day light hours.

At the time Uncle Mitt joined up, flyers had to complete 25 missions before they could go home on a short furlough. Not much later, the rules were changed and that number was upped to 30 missions. Uncle Mitt was on his 29th mission when his Flying Fortress was hit and he heard the command "Abandon Airplane!" He jumped through the tail exit and landed on soft pine needles. He wandered the forest for hours. Eventually, he came to a clearing where his crewmates were hanging from trees. He cut them down. They were all dead.

Uncle Mitt looked for Freedom Fighters but saw none. German soldiers picked him up and took him to the most notorious stalag of the war. He was there almost three years. He never talked about what he saw or experienced. When he came home he was ninety pounds lighter, bent in body and spirit. He did not live to his life expectancy.

World War II was the war to end all wars. Where is our respect for the men and women who died or were maimed in that war ... or in the wars we are fighting now? Stores used to be closed on Veteran's Day and Memorial Day. Stores are open now, luring people in with the biggest sales of the year.

Why don't I see many flags flying now?
When did the pride in our country disappear?
Where did our patriotism go?
Down into the trenches of Vietnam?
Was it Korea or the suicide bombers of Iraq?
What are we doing to get our pride back?
Where is respect for our soldiers and our country?
Where are the flags?

What would GeeGee say?

LONG BEACH

Part One:
Long Beach Junior High

The boardwalk was almost deserted in winter when school was in session. A group of us would study on the benches. How glorious that was! That's when I started to smoke. That's also where I discovered boys and they discovered me. It was Erwin who taught me to kiss until my knees grew weak. I realize now that twelve was too young for all this. There I was, a smoking, kissing kid, and not even a teenager.

You have to live on a northern beach through a winter to realize how beautiful it is. The sky is a neutral calming gray. The Atlantic's high gray waves with their white lacy caps join the sky at the horizon. We are wrapped in a safe cocoon.

Then come the dangerous winter storms. The winds reach hurricane strength and snow is swirled into drifts. Roads are icy. Schools and businesses close. The snow-clearing equipment comes out and heaps the snow into high mounds. When the streets are cleared, businesses and schools open.

Walking to school was an adventure after a blizzard. The streets were icy and slippery and I would land on my bum at least once each winter. The snow hills were lofty. Every one of us would scamper up as high as we could without sinking down into the snow. The world was white and clean, as though it had been washed by the sea. There were no muddy footprints; dogs had not yet been let out to soil the snow. The world looked virginal and pure.

Long Beach Junior High, in New York, was on the bay. Through the large windows, we could see the weather come in with a roar and settle to a murmur.

School came easily for me, except for math. I got zero-minus-one on an exam because I had the date wrong. Chorus and swimming were a respite from boredom. The school had an indoor pool! We could swim all year.

The Flannagans lived across the street from us. Mr. F. had a bed and breakfast with an elegant bar downstairs. He always closed everything down after the summer season. My 13th birthday was coming up in January and, as a gift, he gave me the bar for the evening. All the liquor was stored away for the winter. We could have all the soft drinks we wanted AND he would fix the jukebox so we wouldn't have to use our own nickels. The dance floor was large and Mr. F. waxed it well. What a gift!

Bubby planned the menu and ordered a huge sheet cake for the fifty friends I had invited. Bubby, GeeGee, Mr. F. and some of the other neighbors would be there. Then the calls started coming. Parents would not allow their children to go to a bar. They were furious we would even consider including their children in such wickedness.

So, we had about fifteen kids. *Mam'selle* and *Zippity-Do-Dah* were the hit songs of the night. Leftover cake was wrapped up for me to take to school on Monday for those who couldn't attend. After all, it wasn't their fault.

I was finally in my teens! I thought my whole life would change, but you know how that is....

Winter turned into spring. Brown grass turned green and perennial flowers popped up, adding their joy to the season.

It was a bright April day. As I approached the house, I saw many cars parked in front. Immediately, I knew what had happened. GeeGee had died.

I ran into the house. "Where's Bubby?" I sobbed. At once, I was in her arms.

"Don't worry, Mahshelleh. We are a pair no matter what happens in our world," she crooned, brushing my hair with her palm.

According to custom, GeeGee had to be buried the next day. The house was prepared for Shiva, the seven-day mourning period for the immediate family. Mirrors were covered. Wooden crates were found for the family to sit on. A huge pitcher of water was placed at the front door with many towels. Everyone coming from the cemetery had to wash their hands before entering the house. From the moment Shiva preparation began, no one in the immediate family was permitted to do anything for the entire week. Food would be brought in by family and friends. Dishes, cleaning and household chores would be taken over by others. Ten men would come to pray every morning and evening. An area had to be set for them where they could have drinks and food.

I was preparing to sit Shiva when I was told I was not part of the immediate family. Only spouses, children and siblings could sit. As a grandchild, I was too far down the line, even though they had legally adopted me! I was not permitted to honor GeeGee or grieve publicly for him.

During Shiva, there was always too much food and not enough space. It seemed that everyone who ever knew GeeGee came to pay their respects.

After seven days, it was as if a tap had been turned off. The house was quiet and empty, except for Aunt Anne, Bubby and me. The mirrors were uncovered and the crates taken away. Aunt Anne went home and Bubby and I finally had a chance to sit down and talk.

We had to decide where to live. We had several options. We could go to Glen Cove so we would be closer to Aunt Anne. We could go back to Floral Park and live in one of the apartments. We could stay in Long Beach. After discussion of all the pros and cons, we decided to stay in Long Beach. I was happy that was our choice.

By now, I had been away from school for more than a week. I wanted to stay home one more week. I didn't want to leave Bubby alone all day. I could hear her sobbing at night and I didn't want her to cry all day. But Bubby, always practical, said I had to go back. "It's the end of April and school finishes in June. It's almost over. I'll be all right," Bubby whispered in my ear as we held each other tight. She had a lot of company every day. Friends and neighbors came by, and Aunt Anne made the 45-minute drive at least four times a week.

I forced myself to be cheerful. I would walk home from school along the water with friends. We would sing and joke until we got closer to my house. Then I would shut down, wondering how I could malign GeeGee's memory so quickly. The hole in my chest that GeeGee left was filling with concrete.

I would go into the house to get and give Bubby hugs. She always had a visitor. Whoever it was, they usually waited for me to come home from school.

But GeeGee's chair was always empty.

Part Two:
Last Days in Long Beach

Labor Day was the next weekend. The autumn flowers were starting to bloom and the leaves were changing, but the grass was still green. The Atlantic continued its endless pursuit of the shore. This would be my last year in Junior

High and I fully intended to attend Long Beach Senior High.

The summer had been okay. Aunt Anne, Mara and Harv came, as usual. Bubby and I had been so lonely since GeeGee died, and it was nice to have them with us. But I know it was hard for them. GeeGee was Aunt Anne's father and Mara's, and Harv's grandfather. We were becoming accustomed to his absence, but they did not know the house without GeeGee in it.

Uncle Lou, I am sorry to say, still joined us on weekends. I tried to be away from the house as much as I could but I had to be home before dark. What happened does not seem bad, although I would run crying from the room. It would start innocently enough with a little tickling. Then I would be down on the floor being tickled everywhere. The older I got, the worse the tickling got. Everyone would be sitting around the living room and there I would be, on the floor, laughing and crying hysterically. This was 65 years ago. No one knew the words "inappropriate touching" or "child abuse." The entire family thought it was funny until I got up and ran, sobbing, to my room. I could hear Uncle Lou say, "I don't know what's wrong with her. What did I do?"

Finally, at dinner one night, I gathered all my brave. I said, "I don't like it when Uncle Lou tickles me and I do not want him to do it anymore. It makes me ashamed and embarrassed." Whenever he started again, Bubby

146

would say, "Louie, don't do that anymore. It's not nice." After a couple of attempts, he never tickled me again.

School started after Labor Day weekend. Class clubs were being formed and offices were up for election. I ran for secretary and was elected. My campaign slogan was "I'll keep minutes by the hour." I was still in the chorus and on the swim team.

I had made many friends the previous year and those friendships grew strong. Every so often I would pinch myself when I realized how lucky I was. My family loved me and took care of me. Especially Bubby and GeeGee. Although I was an orphan, I was surrounded by love.

Right after Christmas break, the school gave the chorus a treat for working so hard during the fall and throughout the holiday season. We were taken by bus to a very nice restaurant where we had a super dinner. We even had our choice of desserts. There was a musical quartet and a dance floor. We danced for a while and it was time to get back on the bus. We were dropped off at our houses. It was after eleven when I got home.

There was a strange sound coming from Bubby's room, a croaky, gurgling sound. I went in. Her skin was an odd color, sort of an ashen yellow, and her eyes could not seem to follow me. Every time she breathed, the gurgling sound happened again. Bubby was trying to tell me something, but only that awful sound came out. I ran to the phone to call the doctor and asked her to come right away. She did not ask what was wrong, but was at the door in less than ten minutes. Dr. Crone went directly to Bubby. She asked me to stay in the living room. I could still hear Bubby – by now the sound was a long, continuous gurgle, almost like a raspy sigh. I learned later it was the "death rattle."

In a few minutes, Dr. Crone came out of Bubby's room, put her arm around me and said, "I'm so sorry. She was at peace and didn't suffer. I'm going to find someone to stay with you for the rest of the night."

Mrs. Benoit lived one street over and was at the house in moments. We lit a fire and sat quietly. It was not to be believed that Bubby lay dead in the next room. By now, it was almost one a.m. Mrs. Benoit suggested I call Aunt Anne and Uncle Mitt. I refused, saying they should get a good night's sleep.

I called them at six and soon the house began to fill up. Arrangements needed to be made for Bubby's funeral and for Shiva. Again, I was not permitted to participate because I was not "immediate family."

Once the funeral and Shiva were over, there was still one problem: Me. Where would I live?

It was decided that Aunt Rose (whom I liked) would stay with me till school was out in June. Then I would go to Glen Cove to live with Aunt Anne, Mara, Harv and Uncle Lou.

What would that be like?

AN OVERNIGHT STAY

There are some things I will never forget. Like the night I was arrested.

I was in bed watching television. There was a banging at the door. "Who could be making all that racket?" I asked myself. I threw on a robe and ran to the door. I looked through the peephole to see a police officer. "He's safe," I said to myself.

When the door opened he asked, "Marsha Gordon?" I nodded my head. "I have a summons for your arrest."

My knees buckled as I racked my brain, trying to think what this could be about. I had never committed a crime. It couldn't have been the sliding stop last week. That was the absolute worst thing I could think of.

"You'll find out at the station. Let's go." He read me my rights. After a lot of begging and an equal amount of denial, I realized there was no use continuing this game. We would go and I'd find out what this was all about.

"I'll just change out of my pajamas."

"No, I don't have a female officer to guard you." He handcuffed me and put me into the back seat of the police car, holding my head as I got in. I scrunched down in the seat so none of my neighbors would see me.

Off we went to the Fort Lauderdale Police Station. Still in my pajamas and robe, I was put into a holding cell where I was kept for a long time. I still did not know why I was in jail.

'My' officer came to get me. By now, in my mind, I was calling him Gee Officer Krupke. "We have to go to Daytona Beach. That's where the charges were filed."

It's almost a four-hour drive from Fort Lauderdale to Daytona Beach which gave me the opportunity to ask a lot of questions. I got no answers. Finally, I convinced myself the wrong person had been arrested. We got to Daytona a little after midnight.

Our first stop at the Daytona Beach Police Station was Night Court. Not at all like the old TV program. I finally was told what I was charged with. I had written a check for $3,000 and it had bounced. Now I knew what had happened. My plea was "not guilty"... not that it mattered. I was held over until morning for arraignment.

At last I got out of my pajamas and robe and was issued an orange uniform. I wanted my pajamas back. I had grabbed my purse as Gee Officer Krupke and I were leaving the house. Now it and all its contents were taken from me.

Then processing began. Fingerprinting was first. Starting with the right thumb, the finger pad is rolled in ink, and then pressed onto a card, which designates the fingers of each hand. The thumb is then cleaned of all ink and the right index finger is rolled on the inkpad. On it goes for all ten fingers.

Then it was time for "the picture." I stood up against the wall and a number was put across my chest. Click, click and that was done.

A matron took me to the women's section where I had a private cell. Now, there's an oxymoron. There is nothing private about a cell. The walls and doors are bars. Everyone can hear what you say and see what you do. "Private" means you don't have anyone else in your cell.

Before the matron left, I asked if I could have a snack and coffee. "Yes, ma'am, cream and sugar? We're known for our room service," she said sarcastically. The hoots from the other cells made me realize I'd have nothing to eat tonight. Before the matron left, I asked for a lawyer and gave her a name.

The night was long. The lights, although dimmed from the daytime glare, were still bright. The unmistakable sounds and sighs from the other cells made me glad I was in a "private" cell.

My husband had left me several weeks before all this happened. The first couple of nights he sent flowers and tried to come home. Absolutely not! He was now on his way to Phoenix.

We had a very successful steakhouse on the boardwalk in Hollywood Beach, Florida. Beej was an amazing restaurateur. The Hollywood Steakhouse had not been open a year and had already earned almost a million dollars. He had done this before – run away when he had created a success.

Before he left, he told me he had opened an account for steakhouse bills and not to worry, there was plenty of money in the bank. We owed the meat supplier $3,000 for that week's meat. That was the first check I wrote. When the bounce notification came, I called the bank. The account had been opened with $25!

I should have realized that would be the case. He was the most charming man I had ever met. He could charm the pants off everyone, and he did. He had no sense of responsibility and probably would not realize he had done anything wrong. Where is he now? No one knows if he is dead or alive.

Daylight crept through the bars and the smells of breakfast wafted down the hall. My breakfast tray was slipped through a slot in the bars. I was not sure I could deal with breakfast: watery scrambled eggs and grits, hard toast and pale, cold coffee.

My attorney arrived a few minutes after the breakfast tray. He was a social friend of ours, but I thought he could make a good case for me. I told him what had happened. I also told him we had spent more than $150,000 with the meat company in the past nine months. He left to make some phone calls.

I saw him next at my arraignment. When my case was called, the judge casually said all charges had been dropped. Wow! Wow! Wow!

I thanked the attorney profusely and used him for my divorce.

I got into my pajamas and robe and Gee Officer Krupke drove me home.

I closed the steakhouse that day.

BEFORE AND AFTER

On the whole, my life has been pretty wonderful, especially after my divorce. Sure, there were a few horrendous episodes. By the time I was three, my parents had died of cancer. They had no time to give me siblings; I'm not sure if that's a loss or a blessing.

Bubby and GeeGee, my grandparents, raised me until I was twelve. GeeGee died when I was eleven, Bubby a short year later. I was alone in the house with her when I heard her death rattle. I called the doctor and she came immediately, but it was too late.

Don't go feeling sorry for me. I was the most spoiled orphan in the history of orphandom. I was given love and comfort and a feeling of belonging. I was also given every material thing you can think of.

I sang for the troops in USO shows at Mitchell Field. I started when I was ten and then, at age eleven, I was doing radio shows with the American Theatre Wing. I was one lucky kid.

My maternal family took good care of me. After Bubby and GeeGee left me, I went to live with Aunt Anne and Uncle Lou and their two children. They were what we called "comfortable," which meant they were rich. Again, I wasn't denied a thing.

I had received a small inheritance from my parents and grandparents. When I finished high school, at 18, I was able to move to the Martha Washington Hotel for Women, a den of antiquity, in New York City. I attended a few classes at NYU and met the most charming man from Winnipeg, Canada. Within a week, we were engaged.

May 25, 1951 was our wedding day. I was 18 and Beej was 24. Were we in love? We thought we were. All the parts fit and it felt good. Wasn't that love? Traditionally, the bride's parents pay for the wedding so I insisted on paying for everything out of my inheritance. It was a large wedding at the Commodore Hotel in New York City, then a very good hotel. The wedding took a healthy chunk of my estate.

We found an efficiency apartment on Riverside Drive in New York City and we both went to NYU. Three months later, I went to see my old family doctor who told me I was expecting a baby.

Now what? Beej was getting an allowance from his dad while he was in school. Would we stay in school? Our place was too small to raise a family. What to do?

Beej wanted to go home to Winnipeg. On the practical side, his family was "comfortable." I liked his dad, who was called 'Volff' by everyone. I didn't like his mom, who was called 'Mother.' Beej's extended family consisted of six uncles and ten aunts ... a boisterous, warm group. It was 'Mother' I was worried about.

We bought an old limousine with bullet holes on one side and a chain that fastened the door on the other. We packed it full of our silver and crystal wedding gifts and started the trip to Winnipeg. My morning sickness lasted all day and I heaved in every state at least once.

We lived in Winnipeg for ten years and all three children were born there. Thank God for them. It was about this time that I felt myself falling into a deep, dark abyss. I was blindly following my Svengali-like husband ... not taking part in my life, losing my self and my being.

We bought a popular nightclub and brought in acts directly from *The Ed Sullivan Show*. That was fine, but Beej got grandiose and bought talent a small city could not support for a week at a time. He was covering expenses with my inheritance – he had total access – and borrowing money from Volff.

Beej was not much of a family man. The children were of passing interest. Challenge and conquest were what kept him going except for the times he hid out in the living room with the drapes drawn and the phones off.

We were broke and so was Volff. We left Winnipeg in the dark of night for New York. This was to become a pattern – we moved twenty times in fifteen years, mostly at night. I finally realized that other women played a huge part in Beej's life from the beginning of our marriage. I can't believe how naïve I was – the money, the moving, the women, the highs, the lows.

We moved from New York to Miami. Whenever 'Mother' came to visit, all my plants died. The 15 years after Winnipeg dragged along, until finally, Beej left me for another woman on July 4th.

That became my personal Independence Day.

Although he wanted to come back, I realized that would not be good for the children or for me. I divorced him, getting no alimony, no child support – just my freedom and a clean slate.

After the divorce, I found a new person – me! I made good decisions. I found good jobs, traveled and enjoyed wonderful adventures. I had two long-term relationships, one for twelve years and one for ten. For the first time in my life, I was happy and carefree.

I loved being me!

Changing Diapers

Babies change our lives in so many ways.

Mothers' Helpers
Farts
Potty Patter

MOTHERS' HELPERS

For Canadian women in the 1950s, birthing a baby was as easy as falling off a log.

This was my first baby and I asked the doctor if it was going to hurt. "Don't worry about a thing, Little Mother. We're going to take care of everything." And so they did. I was put to sleep and when I awoke, I held beautiful Gary in my arms.

Mothers and infants stayed in the hospital at least a week, more if they wanted to. We came home to three starched nurses, one for every eight hours. They stayed for a minimum of three weeks and were territorial as far as the babies were concerned.

The night nurse was angry with me. I was nursing Gary and asked Nurse to bring him to me for his night feedings. No, she wouldn't do that. She asked me to put a bottle of my milk in the refrigerator so she could feed him. Come on, I wasn't Elsie the Cow. I wanted Gary for his night feedings and that was that. I'm sure she thought she would be fired because I didn't need a night nurse. She didn't understand how structured the young mothers of Winnipeg were. We all had money and shopped the same shops. Our meat came from the same butcher and our groceries came from the Hudson's Bay Company which delivered in snow, sleet and storm. No way would any of us fire a nurse. This would cast doubt about whether the nurses were needed by anyone.

After three weeks of nurses, the mothers' helpers immediately filled the vacuum. The helpers were traditionally country girls who wanted to complete their education in the city. They helped with the babies, maybe washed the dinner dishes. They sought room and board and a small allowance in return.

My father-in-law was the Baron land owner in Canada. He had miles and miles of bushland (forest) which was home to two Indian reservations. About the bushland: no one can ever buy it. The land is leased for 99 years with an automatic renewal. Those 99 years seemed so far into the future back then. It's almost here....

Lonya was the first to come from the reservation. She was about sixteen, clean and scared. She had a quick smile, even in a strange environment. She also had a crush on my husband. She would sit on the living room floor with her head on his knee. She and little Gary were crazy about each other. Lonya left when I discovered Gary had a major lice infestation.

Connie was next off the reservation. She was not quick to adapt to the wonders of life in the city. Each new unbelievable experience took the better part of a week to accept. That such miracles could exist in the world boggled her mind.

The washing machine: We went down to the basement to wash the dirty laundry. We started by sorting the clothes, separating darks from lights. So far, so good. Then we measured the detergent and put that into the machine. I showed Connie how to move the dial and where to stop – and that's when she discovered the window in the washer's door. She ran to get a chair and sat there through the cycles ... every day ... for eight days.

The telephone: Connie was doing well with incoming calls although the ring startled her and she had this funny kangaroo jump. It was time for Connie to make outgoing calls. We stood at the kitchen counter and I explained the dial. She could ignore the letters; we were using only the numbers. We practiced dialing a neighbor's number for a few minutes. When I thought she had it, I asked her to wait five minutes, and then call me at my neighbor's. I got there and waited five, ten, fifteen minutes before going home. Poor girl, there she was at the counter, making the dial go round and round. I had neglected to tell her to pick up the receiver. I accept all responsibility for this one.

Connie had to go back to the reservation in a few weeks. Her grandmother was very ill. That was too bad. I think she would have worked out.

By now we had two children, Gary and Carey Ellen. The mothers' helpers came and went. Some of the other mothers were having luck with a local agency. I gave them a call.

The doorbell rang. I answered it and there was Mary Poppins! Perhaps 50 years older than the other helpers, she had that peaches-and-cream complexion English women are so lucky to have. Her hair was a halo of white and her enunciation was straight from the palace. "Good morning, ma'am. I've come from the agency. My name is Mrs. Lark Worthy."

I wanted to hug her but instead brought her into the house and showed her "her" room. She was delighted and we had a cuppa and talked about the house, the schedule, and the children. Just then, the children came in from playing outside. I introduced them to Mrs. Worthy. Their manners were perfect. I was never so proud.

We were Mrs. Worthy's first clients as a mother's helper. She could not afford to live alone; she had a very meager income. I dreamed of her staying until the children were married.

At the end of the week, she told me this was just too hard for her. She was not accustomed to children anymore. "Oh, and one more thing, ma'am. My name is Rosemary Lark-Worthy, not Mrs. Worthy." Through my tears, I wished her well and hoped we hadn't offended her in any other way.

Kathy Wickster was next to appear on our doorstep. Kathy was in her early 40s, attractive, dark-haired and well dressed. I invited her in and she began flitting about the house; all the bedrooms, the den, kitchen, dining room and baths. She needed her own telephone and would I please have one installed in the morning? Yes, I said to her vanishing back. She spotted the children out back and went out to play with them.

Kathy's first day was Friday so her phone was not installed until Monday. Kathy rarely slept and once she had her phone, she spoke to the all-night talk shows. She also had, from somewhere, the home phone numbers of car salesmen. She started buying cars and, in the morning, a rainbow of cars would be lined up in front of our house. Kathy assured everyone they'd "be taken care of." The dealers started calling us for payment, but we explained we had nothing to do with the purchases.

My favorite way of entertaining has always been small dinner parties, never more than six or eight. Kathy would set a place for herself at the table and then appear in her long, red hostess gown. Although the seating was lopsided and she tended to monopolize the conversation, I just let it go. But there was something wrong here. We were now into Kathy's fifth or sixth week. I was becoming concerned for her and my children.

She started painting. The first was a bloody skull pushed onto a post, all of it under water. Her paintings became more macabre. One morning I walked into the kitchen and there was three-year-old Gary with a huge knife in his hand. Kathy said he needed to learn about bad things sometime.

I called a friend and asked him to drive Kathy to the hospital. Today, I think of Kathy often. Now that I've been diagnosed as bi-polar, I would have understood her a lot better and recognized her problem earlier. She must have been off her meds.

Kathy was our last mothers' helper.

FARTS

My son Gary and the neighbor's boy, Freddie, had been friends forever in their young lives. One day, when the boys were about four, Fred's mother called.

"Hello?"

"Don't 'hello' me, Marsha," said Liz, angrier than I'd ever heard her, even when Freddie painted the wall with his BM. Liz has a low tolerance level.

"Freddie's been running around here the last few days, passing gas and singing, 'It's a happy. I'm a happy. Happys are fun and good for you.' Freddie says that's what you do at your house. Have you lost your mind?"

Flatulence is the medical term for passing gas. It's a difficult word for children. "Passing gas" made me think I was driving by a Texaco station. Since "fart" was not a socially acceptable word in the 50s, we decided to call *them* "happys."

I never could convince Liz this was a healthy attitude. She limited the time the boys spent together. After all, who knew what else I would come up with?

Flash ahead 52 years. I am now 76. Those of us who have reached this lofty age know we fart. Always curious, I decided to research farts. Three dictionaries gave me no leads. I googled 'fart' and received numerous entries. I chose Facts on Farts, which printed out 28 pages of valuable information. What kind of spam do you think I'll get?

The gas in our intestines comes from the air we swallow and from gas that seeps into our intestines from our blood. Bacteria living in our guts also produce hydrogen and methane. Air comes into our bodies when we mouth-breathe or chew gum. This additional air creates more gas, thereby giving us a greater propensity for farting. These gases, and foods such as cauliflower, eggs and meat, are known for producing smelly farts. Beans produce large amounts of not-so-stinky farts.

An average person produces about half a liter of gas a day, distributed over an average of 14 daily farts.

Some people say they never fart. Not true – if they are alive, they fart. Women fart just as much as men do. Men are simply prouder of their farts, to the point of having contests.

If you fart in a large group of people, act oblivious, or look quickly at the person next to you as though you know he did it.

In our house, we do not need to do that. Happys are not embarrassing; they are happy. (Fart is still not a socially acceptable word.)

Today, as I look fondly at my children, there is happiness all around us.

POTTY PATTER

There are two times in life when the main topic of conversation is bowel movements: infancy and senior adulthood.

A baby's bowel movement is of significant importance to parents both before and after potty training. It forms the basis for many conversations with many people.

At the other end of the spectrum, senior conversations with friends are based mostly on their health, with bowels leading the way. A typical senior phone conversation might sound like this:

"Hello?"

"Hello. Are you still constipated?"

"Yes, it's been six days," I say shyly.

"Don't worry about a thing. I once went twelve days without moving my bowels and no impaction," he says with pride.

Here is where this call deviates from the typical:

"Listen, Paul," I say. "I've been thinking – I don't want to talk about poop anymore. Every conversation centers on our bowels. Now, I know I'm supposed to ask you, 'How's it going? Still problems with unexpected movements while you're away from home?' But I want to talk about current events, other people, even the weather.

Starting this minute, I'm through with all this crap."

"Uh, well, okay. Umm... It's going to rain this afternoon but right now, it's a beautiful day. Do you think Obama's doing a good job? Jess, I can't do this. You're a good friend. I really want to know how you are."

"My body has other anatomical parts, other than my bowels. Like my brain, for instance."

"Okay, I'll try. We'll see how it all comes out."

Another call, this time from Mary.

"Hi, Jess. Still constipated?"

"Mary, I just had this out with Paul. No longer am I talking about any body irregularities, specifically bowels. I want to talk about current affairs, news of the world. Just because we're getting older doesn't mean we have to live in this tight little cocoon. We need to exercise our brains."

"Well, all right, Mrs. Feelgood. See if I care how you are." She hung up.

And so it goes, at least in my little crowd of senior citizens. Certainly, as individuals, we care about the debt and presidential candidates. However, as a group, seniors can't get past their bowels.

Changing Minds

*Mankind's gentle dreams,
how quickly they turn into nightmares!
(Donald Duck)*

Cousin Harvey
Depression
Diffusing Anger
I Can't Think of a Title

COUSIN HARVEY

Preface:
Hummin' Along

I met Jennie on a cruise ship and I will never forget her.

She was traveling with her daughter and son-in-law, as was I. One night we were assigned to the same dinner table. Jennie had Alzheimer's and did not speak much. Her smile was enigmatic. She was able to walk with the aid of a cane and could feed herself. Jennie was in her mid-eighties and had served as a military nurse during World War II. She turned her incomprehensible smile toward me. I asked if she remembered the war. She emphatically nodded her head. I asked other questions but either no reply was given or she shook her head as if she was shouting, "No!"

Time to get on with the war, I thought. Quietly I began to sing:

> "Comin' in on a wing and a prayer,
> Though there's one motor gone
> We can still carry on;
> We're comin' in on a wing and a prayer."

It was here that I realized there was a soft humming next to me, perfectly in tune. I continued and so did Jennie's humming:

"We're comin' in on a wing and a prayer,
With our full crew aboard
And our trust in the Lord,
We're comin' in on a wing and a prayer."

Jennie sang the last line with me. She looked astonished and clapped her hands softly, bowing her head in acknowledgment of our applauding dinner mates.

Part One

My cousin Harv was in his early 50s when Arlene sensed something was wrong. They went to specialists and the unanimous diagnosis was Early Onset Alzheimer's. The disease progressed rapidly. It has been at least ten years since Harv has recognized Arlene or his sons. He doesn't speak now, nor can he walk. He is incontinent and needs to be fed. He always hated bananas and milk. Now he eats anything he is given. His body is healthy. His mind is gone.

Harv is seven years younger than I am. I lived with him, his sister, Aunt Anne and Uncle Lou during my high school years. I have been in awe of him, I believe, since he came home from the hospital, wrapped in a blue baby blanket. Everything came easily to Harv. He teethed early. His grade point average was always the highest. He was on the football team. He was a lifeguard and became a Manhattan attorney high in a skyscraper's corner office.

He appreciated the hand life dealt him. He grew up, married Arlene and had three loving sons.

Arlene and the boys have a hope. They hope Harv will recognize me. So tomorrow, I am off to Westchester. My hope is for a hum-along with Harv. I pray our hopes are not dashed.

Part Two

I went to see Cousin Harv last weekend. He is in a locked Alzheimer's unit in an assisted living facility.

The plane from Fort Myers is completely full – families with many small children. This was the first time I heard children's voices ask, "Are we down yet?" Whatever happened to "Are we there yet?"

We have a moment of turbulence and from the cockpit, the pilot's voice commands, "Ladies and Gentlemen, hold on to your babies."

Arlene meets me in the baggage claim area in the airport. We both cry, kiss and hug each other. I think we hold on to one another for the strength we will need for this weekend.

We go to the house to drop off my things. Arl's and Harv's house is my favorite anywhere. It wraps its arms around me and comforts me from the moment I walk in the door. It's just that kind of place.

It is time to see Harv – less than a ten-minute drive from the house. We enter the

175

building and take the elevator to the sixth floor. There are combination locks everywhere. We look for Harv and find him on the patio. It is a magnificent day; temperature in the low 70s, no humidity and a delightful breeze.

There is Harv, sitting with Cynthia, his caregiver.

Oh, God, he looks wonderful; still Handsome Harv. Straight and tall in his chair. Dressed impeccably, he could be on his way to the golf course. I see adoration in his eyes when he looks at Arl. She does not think it is so.

Now, he is looking at a distant place. His empty eyes are expressionless.

It takes a while for Harv to notice me. I smile. He smiles back. I sit next to him. He takes my hand and holds it.

Does he really take my hand? Or is the grasp a result of a side effect of Alzheimer's? It attacks the nerve cells in the brain and spinal cord. This results in spastic gestures over which he has no control. I simply know I like Harv holding my hand, whatever the reason.

We remain on the patio for a couple of hours. Then Harv wriggles in his chair, trying to stand up. An attendant takes Harv back to his room in his wheelchair. He needs to be changed. Harv, what has happened to you? What is this horrid disease that has stolen your life?

Arlene and I wait in the hall. We go to his room when he is presentable. Arl sprays room freshener everywhere. The room is homey. Harv does not have a roommate and Arl has used her gift for decorating to make it comfortable for mind and body. Family pictures, hundreds of them, fill corkboards that line the walls. Arlene has brought the family to Harv.

A large bed takes up one corner of the room. Across from the bed is a purple couch. Two great big leather chairs and many tables make up the rest of the comfortable room. A new, large television sits across from one of the chairs. A small refrigerator holds treats and drinks for Harv... including a bottle of bourbon.

It is almost dinnertime and Arlene wants to be certain Harv is fed. Cynthia had gone home when we arrived. It seems the facility attendants are so accustomed to Cynthia doing everything for Harv, they sometimes forget to feed him.

Harv is wheeled into the dining room. We follow. He is transferred to a dining room chair. We wait for his food. When Cynthia is there, she goes into the kitchen and gets his dinner. He is last to be served tonight, almost as an afterthought. It takes a long time for a person to come feed him. When the attendant gets there she feeds Harv with her right hand, and the patient next to him with her left. Not much personal attention here. Harv opens his mouth when the fork comes close and keeps his mouth closed when he has had enough. No amount of coaxing will open his mouth, like a petulant child.

Arl and I go back to his room and see Harv settled for the rest of the evening. We kiss him.

He smiles and we each say, "I love you." Harv looks adoringly at Arl and smiles a small smile. I tell Harv I will see him tomorrow and then I will go home to Florida. Arlene gives him a shot of bourbon. He would have a little scotch or bourbon each night before he went to sleep at home. He licks his lips.

Arl and I go home and I sleep in what was to have been Harv's home office. I feel him in the room, perhaps in my dreams.

Arlene wants to see Harv at lunchtime. We get there just as he is eating. The day is getting hot and humid so we go to Harv's room instead of the patio. The attendant says he has been crying all morning.

Why? Because he wants to be home with Arlene? Because I am going home?

I cry as I tell Harv how much I love him. Harv is now crying with me. I tell him how grateful I am for his kindness to me. I tell him how much his love means to me. Does he know me? Or am I just a nice person who has come to visit?

I do not know. I know it was important for me to see him.

This trip was for me.

DEPRESSION

I am in that place again. I am depressed.

I sit in my chair, shoulders hunched up to my ears. There is pressure in my head and in my chest.

The telephone is wedged between my thigh and the arm of the chair. The television remote is in my right hand. A book is overturned on my lap. I want nothing to do with these things and shove them onto the floor.

It is three in the afternoon. I am still in my pajamas, my hair not combed, my teeth not brushed.

I turn off the fan. I want no interaction with anyone or anything. I don't *want* to be comfortable.

I am deep in the nether regions of a depression.

I am not speaking to anyone.

I am not leaving my house.

I am making no decisions.

I am taking no responsibility.

I am bi-polar.

They used to call it manic-depression. That made sense to me. You were either flying higher than a soaring bird or down in a deep, black hole. You *knew* if you were manic or depressed.

Then the medical mavens changed the name of the illness to bi-polar. Like someone who travels between Alaska and the Antarctic. I cannot identify with the new name.

My manic state is relatively mild. I am able to keep several balls in the air with great aplomb and success. I love manic.

My depressed state is severe. As I sit in my chair, I see broken pieces of my life littering the living room floor. I feel slighted by casual social remarks and situations real or imagined. I am devastated by world events and politics.

Medication helps keep me level, but every once in a while, depression creeps in. I dig up old resentments and dwell on them. Digging the hole makes it deeper. I want to wallow in it.

Then I remember. My doctor has upped one of my meds. It helps, and that gives me a measure of hope.

I am in that place again. But I do not have to stay here.

DIFFUSING ANGER

Deep in the throes of a depression, my therapist told me, "Depression is anger turned inward." He went on to say, "Identify the anger and confront it."

There was a time when I would write, on a small piece of paper, the anger I was feeling. Then I would crumble the paper, place it in the kitchen sink, put a match to it and burn it to ashes. It was effective.

I cannot do that anymore. Every room in this condominium, including the kitchen, is equipped with a sprinkler system. Water comes cascading down at the slightest hint of smoke. An alarm goes off in the fire station. An automatic message comes over the loudspeakers in every apartment, "Evacuate the building." The fire trucks' sirens wail as they approach the property. The evacuation call continues, commanding us all to leave our homes.

I needed to find a new ritual. Someone suggested I write letters to the people who caused my anger, but not mail them. That didn't work.

I shredded the letters. Didn't help. I was still depressed.

I identified my current angers and listed them numerically in order of importance. Then I worked on each one ... my depression was diminishing.

I decided to go back as far as I could remember and remove all the angry memories from my mind.

Four years old: I was angry with my grandfather for not buying me my own seat for the circus at Madison Square Garden. He thought I would be frightened by the big crowds and would feel safer on his lap. I thought he was cheap.

I went to kindergarten. Joanie Kowolski did not invite me to her birthday party. We lived next door to each other and had been best friends since birth. But Joanie went to parochial school and I went to public school. She invited her whole class to her party. Perhaps I didn't fit in with her new friends.

I don't remember any other anger until fourth grade. Louie Bono was in my class; he was the biggest bully in the school. In the cafeteria one day, he tried to push ahead of me in line. I told him he would have to wait his turn. He just laughed, so I poured a bowl of tomato soup over his head. Oh, I was furious with Louie Bono!

I continued on through my life looking for old anger, writing each one I found on a list. Now I had two lists: current angers, which I had already confronted successfully, and the list of 43 old angers that I started to work on.

The list is a wonderful idea. It works! The old angers that clouded my outlook are disappearing.

Except for Joanie Kowolski and Louie Bono. I can't seem to let go of those memories.

Maybe I'll take a chance and burn them in the sink.

I CAN'T THINK OF A TITLE

My mind is as blank as a newly erased blackboard. Clouds of white chalk dust float across the board. Ephemeral thoughts race through my mind, elusive, unstoppable, uncatchable.

This is the day I have been dreading. I cannot dredge up a story idea. Goodness knows I have tried. I have titles: *The Sum of All My Parts, Cloud Thoughts, The Man in Green.* Perhaps one day I will be able to flesh them out. I am going to sit here until my fingers find the computer keys and my mind finds a topic.

But first, I'll throw in some laundry.

Okay, I'm back at the computer, sitting and thinking, thinking and sitting. Nothing comes to mind. But I am going to sit here for the next half-hour and then another half-hour and so the day shall pass and I *will* write.

I need to empty the dishwasher. Then I will start my half-hour.

I am now into the second half-hour, squirming in my desk chair. This is silly. I might as well pay some bills while I am just sitting here.

The third half-hour just started and I am not even getting up. I know the second half-hour does not count. I was busy paying the utility companies and charge cards and writing checks for things I did not need.

Now, I am going to sit here and think. Here come the ephemeral ideas again, racing, teasing, flitting through my mind. Doesn't matter, one of them will stick.

What was that noise? The washing machine is finished. I will put the clothes in the dryer.

I will take out the trash.

I will make my bed.

I will clean the fridge.

I will not have a story this week.

Changing Clothes

Beware of all enterprises that require new clothes.
(Henry David Thoreau)

The Funeral
My Closet
Shoelaces

187

THE FUNERAL

Hal died a few months after I visited him. I chose not to go to the funeral for two reasons: One, I had recently seen him; and two, the Friendly family made me gag.

The Friendlys were movie star rich. They would use Hal's funeral to show off to each other, just as they use every occasion. Robbie would show up in his Rolls Royce and his wife in her Lamborghini. They went everywhere in both cars. The cemetery road would be cluttered with Porsches, Mercedes, Jags and an Aston Martin.

The men would wear hand sewn Seville Row and Italian overcoats. Their winter boots would be Fiorentini and Baker, starting at $800 a pair. The women would keep warm in chinchilla and ermine; forget mink for this crowd. Their boots would be Manola Blahnk at a minimum of $1,000 a pop.

Abby, Hal's wife, called me afterwards and confirmed all this. She said it looked like opening night at the Met. The diamonds outshone the sun. Because of the glare, the clergyman had a problem reading the service.

I am glad I didn't go in my raincoat with the removable winter lining and my $35 (on sale) boots.

I hate it when I think like that.

Rest in peace, Hal.

MY CLOSET

Picture my closet. It's a big square.
Tops are on one side.
Pants are on the other.
Short sleeved blouses.
Long sleeved tops.
Long pants.
Crop pants and pedal pushers.
Broad categories are separated by color.
Jackets, vests and sweaters are together, separately.
Then there are coats.

Shoes *were* color-coded, in concert with the color that hung above them. I could not remain *that* organized. Shoes now march randomly across the closet floor. None of them are in step. Pairs are not together.

My shoes are a clue to what my closet used to be like. Blouses, each hung onto hangers by one shoulder. Colors ran together like a kindergarten water painting. Forget long sleeves, short sleeves. Forget long pants, crop pants. No piece of clothing had any claim to closet real estate. It was every piece for itself. Empty space? Hang it there.

There were just two points of organization: all hangers faced the same way. The second point has to do with wearing clothes twice before they were laundered. Before I washed clothes, I turned them inside out. I hung them up that way in my closet so I knew I had not worn them since they had been laundered.

Everything is right side out now. I don't wear my clothes twice anymore.

How did my closet go from ridiculous to sublime?

I moved into new housing and asked my son, Gary, and his wife, Beth, to help me settle in. They came up from Key West to help Mom. I had specific chores for them. Beth was to repot plants and organize my closet. Beth is an organizer *par excellence*. She looked in my closet and shuddered. I know I *look* organized on the outside, but what a tangled mass I am on the inside.

It has been about six months since Beth created calm out of chaos. Gary called me the other day. I could hear Beth in the background. "Ask Marsha how her closet looks."

I answered, "Tell Beth I tried to hang a white pair of pants with the navy pants. I heard sobbing from the closet and all the other pants wound their legs around each other. I put the white pants with the other white pants and they all calmed down. Tell Beth the closet is in sync and still looks terrific."

I could not tell her about the shoes.

SHOELACES

I had a senior moment the other day. I forgot how to tie my laces.

My frustration as a three year old stays with me to this day. My grandmother, whose middle name should have been Patience, worked with me. I would "get it" and the next day I'd forget it. Grandma calmly started again until I was able to tie my shoes for the rest of my life. At least, until now. My children went through the same angst until the day came when the whole family could tie their shoes.

Used to be that children were taught to tie their shoes between ages three and five. Today, the age is between four and six. Why? Velcro. Velcro and zippers, flip-flops and moccasins.

No shoelaces until we get to sneakers. Sneakers happen when Mom decides that tiny feet look so cute in tiny sneakers. Or when the child becomes sports-minded or fashion-conscious, usually around five or six years old.

And the whole learning process begins again, with a new generation.

Mathematicians tell us there are two trillion ways of putting the laces through the eyelets. *Ian's Shoelace Site,* on the Internet, offers 33 different ways to lace up shoes. One is the "Two Loop Shoelace Knot," also known as the "Bowknot" or "Bunny Ears:"

Step 1. Tie a Left-over-Right Starting Knot, and then make both ends into loops by doubling them back onto themselves. *This is assuming I know how to tie a left-over-right knot. Why can't it be right over left? I can do that.*

Step 2. Cross the two loops over each other so that the right loop ends up in front and the left loop ends up behind. The left loop is now the right loop. *Is that even possible? I know I'm lost and have to go back to Step 1. But you can go on to Step 3.*

Step 3. Begin to wrap the right loop ... *which right?* ... around the left loop to end up in front.

Step 4. Start to feed the right loop into the "hole" that has just been made. *There is no hole. Where is the hole?*

Step 5. With the right loop now through the hole, grab both loops and start to pull the knot tight. Hooray! You have tied your shoe! *Not me. I'm still on Step 1.*

Those are the instructions with which you teach your children to tie their shoes. And we haven't even tried putting the laces through the eyelets.

Okay, think learning to tie laces was hard? We are now going to buy laces. Our choices used to be white, black or brown. Now we can buy all colors of the rainbow plus every transmutation thereof. There are plaid laces, stripes, polka dots and glow-in-the-dark laces. There are canvas laces and denim laces, stretch laces and curly laces. *I feel a chill go through my body. The thought of bunny ears and curly laces is more than I can bear.*

A major decision: I am buying shoes with Velcro for all my grandchildren. What about me? Am I getting Velcro shoes for me?

No way! I am getting magenta polka dot shoelaces and cannot wait to tie one on.

Changing Tires

Be sure your spare is properly inflated
– a life lesson.

Nobody Reads on the Bus
Into the Wild Blue Yonder

NOBODY READS ON THE BUS

The ferry trip to Key West was serene. The water was calm, the wind arrived in gentle puffs, the temperature was a perfect 75 degrees. I finished my book and concentrated on my suntan. I anticipated, with much peace, my week in Key West.

However, within three days the Keys were on hurricane watch. Mandatory evacuation, especially for tourists, was announced. In the twelve years I lived in Key West I had never evacuated, but now I felt I must. Perhaps the word "tourist" did it. After all, that's what I was now.

I called the airlines; no seats left. They were discontinuing flights anyway in about an hour. The weather convinced the Key West Ferry folks to cancel service for several days.

The only transportation out of town was the Greyhound bus. I picked up magazines and a book to read for the eight hour road trip back to Fort Myers. I remembered from so long ago that everyone read on the bus.

It had been a long time since I'd traveled on a Greyhound Bus. Probably 50 years. I wasn't sure what to expect. The bus was clean and comfortable and there was plenty of leg room. The seat reclined and the personal overhead light and a/c worked. Much more comfortable and far cleaner then I remembered.

A mélange of passengers waited inside the surprisingly clean bus depot at the airport. Diego, the driver, said there were twice as many passengers this morning, and more gringos than ever.

Boarding and luggage loading started at 8:30 on this cloudless morning. Most passengers kept their luggage with them: overfilled shopping bags, duffles with straps missing, coats and sweaters hung over their arms on this hot Florida day. Some of these passengers were dark haired and brown skinned; some were blonde and blue-eyed. All had the same look of lost in their eyes. They spoke quietly in their native languages. These were hotel and restaurant workers leaving Key West where "affordable housing" is an oxymoron. They were leaving due to an economic storm.

Then there were the suspicious "ferry refugees" who watched carefully as Diego put their neat bags into the underbelly of the bus. Suddenly, I realized I was part of this group. When did that happen?

8:45 a.m. and off we went, right on time.

No one was reading so I talked with some of my fellow passengers.

The tall broad Jamaican man with Rasta braids has huge hands that are gentle in our handshake. He is a glass blower working on a Key West motel renovation and is proud of what he's doing. He is headed away from the weather and is eager for the storm to be over so he can get back to his job.

The Canadian teacher comes down to the Keys twice a year for the "flora" and smuggles back samples for his school kids. He loves the islands and hopes someday to retire in the Keys. The Greyhound is his usual mode of transportation to and from the Miami airport. "Cheaper and more comfortable than any other ride, eh?"

Then there's the whistler sitting behind me. Several teeth are missing so his whistle is more of a hissing lisp. Joe lives on the Greyhound bus line. His Greyhound pass allows him to migrate with the birds, south in the winter, north in the summer, east and west whenever. His daughter mails his Social Security check to him wherever he is. This has been a good trip to Key West. His sleep on the beach was uninterrupted. He is clean and explains that he makes regular use of public restrooms and carries grooming supplies and clean clothes in his bag. Every ten days or so, depending on weather, he stays in a motel. Not a bad life....

Jeff boards in Marathon and sits across the aisle. A towering, bearded man, he is headed back to Wyoming to pick up his belongings. His grin is hidden by his beard but visible in his eyes. He has just bought a 27' Hunter sailboat and is planning to live aboard in Key West. Jeff says he's worked hard his whole life and has decided it's time to leave the real world. He's 57.

The bus was filling up. We zipped along to Homestead which was a large air force base first used in 1955. Many military families who served at the base retired in Homestead. I looked around. No one was talking to his neighbor. No one was reading, not even the gringos.

At the bus station, a diverse group of at least 35 waited to board. Migrant workers and Asians outnumbered the retired U.S. military. Everyone got on the bus, but not all had seats. A large Haitian woman in her best blue dress took the last available seat next to me, the gringo lady. After a while I understood she was on her way to Orlando to visit her daughter for two days. A light tan woman stood a few seats in front of me cradling a baby. I gestured that I would hold her infant. She looked startled and turned away, gripping the baby tighter.

The Miami Airport was the next stop. Most of the gringos, except Joe, Jeff and I, got off the bus at the Miami Airport. No new passengers got on.

We continued on to the Miami bus station to transfer to other buses. The station was small and dirty and I was happy to be there in daylight. I was hungry and I was tired and none of the vending machines worked.

Then I met Dennis and we talked for an hour between our buses. He was wearing a blue pinstriped suit and a yellow shirt. His reddish tie was in a perfect Windsor knot. He was on his way to Atlanta where he was going to learn to be the best darn salesman of a new health food product. He would have people buy the product and join his group and then they would sell the health product and he would make money from what they sold. He opened his brand new briefcase. "Want to buy some? It's really healthy."

I remember Dennis with more clarity than I do the other passengers; their tired faces, tired eyes, tired bodies. I think Dennis is my hope for the future.

Maybe he reads on the bus.

INTO THE WILD BLUE YONDER

Why do I fly when I'm in a hurry? On a recent trip to Toronto, I was four hours late reaching my destination. Coming home, I was 27 hours late. That's 31 hours of my life.

I remember when flying was a gracious experience. Women wore hats and gloves; men wore suits and ties. Meals (!) were served on linen-covered trays, dishes were china and flatware was silver plate. The planes were roomy enough to stretch our legs.

The equipment from Fort Myers to Newark must have come from the Smithsonian. Not that it was roomy; heaven forbid. Originally, the plane might have seated twenty. There were sixty passengers crammed into the space.

Anyone remember Uri Geller on the Ed Sullivan show? He would look at a teaspoon with great concentration until the spoon handle bent over the bowl. That is precisely how the seats were shaped. We sat with our backs bent for the two-hour journey. Midway through the trip, the flight attendants served one cookie per passenger and a small drink. The attendants were huffing and puffing with the exertion. Perhaps there is no age limit for flight attendants anymore. We got to Newark with no problems but sore backs.

It was in Newark that the troubles began. An anticipated half-hour layover lasted four hours.

The connecting flight had been misplaced. It had been sent to maintenance the previous day. When they had completed their work, the plane was left for pickup outside in the freezing weather. Maintenance thought it had been picked up and was at the gate. The gate thought it was at maintenance. When the plane was finally found, all liquids had frozen, including the lavatories. The defrosting process began.

I travel with a wheelchair, so I'm first on and last off. Once defrosting began, I was taken to the plane, which sat out in the field. The plane was too small for the jetway. The temperature was 25 degrees and I had packed my coat in my checked luggage. The heat had not yet been turned on in the plane. I asked for a blanket but was told that service is no longer provided.

No longer provided, like many other niceties. This year, airlines have garnered huge, record profits, most of them from service charges paid by the passengers. On some airlines, you can rent a pillow and blanket for $7.50. My one checked bag cost $25.00. A bulkhead seat is $35.00. Crummy lunches start at $8.50. And I sit, shivering, on a cold plane because this carrier no longer provides blankets, not even for rent.

We finally got to Toronto where the temperature was ten degrees. We parked on the tarmac and I still had no coat. No coat and no jetway. But my friends were waiting in the terminal, and a glorious time in Toronto began.

Four days later: time to go home. We called the airport. My flight was delayed because the crew was late. The delay would cause me to miss the connecting flight. This would mean an eight-hour layover in Newark and I wouldn't get home until one the next morning. I chose to leave the following day.

The trip home was uneventful. I carried my coat and had jetways at all transfer points.

Will I ever fly again? Sure I will, complaining all the way.

<u>**Changing Views**</u>

If you never change your mind, why have one?
(Edward deBono)

Dude, Can We Talk?
New-Fangled Unemployment
The Pharmaceutical Rip-off

DUDE, CAN WE TALK?

The cousins sit next to each other on their grandfather's couch. One lives in Oregon. He is ten. The other lives in Connecticut and he is thirteen years old. There they sit together ... texting ... each other!

Advances in communications have resulted in fewer friendships. Young people who have never met face to face are now BFFs (best friends forever). The ability to interact with each other verbally is declining. Among pre-teens and teens, it is becoming uncomfortable to speak directly to another person. The quality of verbal interaction is rapidly deteriorating. Within a few generations, thumbs will evolve into the size of oars.

According to a recent poll by Disney Mobile and Harris Interactive in which they tracked young people's use of texting, 44% said texting is their main form of communication. They text more than they talk! Two out of three students interviewed acknowledged they text during class.

Texters have no rules, no grammar, no spelling. They also have no manners. Teens and pre-teens live in a world of beeps and chirps. They will ignore the physical company they are in and see to their text messages.

Next time you're out, look at groups of two, three, twenty teens. Most will be texting. This is an insult to the people they're actually with. All this empty contact is a waste of time and abilities. Relationships with flesh and blood friends are diffused if the only connection is electronic. Some teens who text are also often on-line, forging dangerous liaisons with electronic stalkers.

What to do? As adults, we do not set good examples. Cell phones are attached to our ears, and some of our thumbs have found the convenience of texting, as well. We have to start somewhere!

<u>How about the dinner table</u>? That same Disney/Harris poll tells us that 25% of teenagers text at the dinner table. I would wager some adults at the table are themselves talking on cell phones or texting. Let's make the dinner table an electronic free zone. Parents, show an interest in the school teams, newspaper, drama club, wherever your kids are active. Check out the latest pre-teen and teen movies. It is going to be up to you to carry the conversational ball. Try not to ask questions that can be answered with 'yes' or 'no'.

Let's talk.

NEW-FANGLED UNEMPLOYMENT

Last month my daughter and I took a road trip to Tampa. As we approached the toll areas, signs proclaimed, "DO NOT STOP – DO NOT PAY TOLL." *How nice, I thought. It must be Motorist Appreciation Day.* This month, my daughter received a bill in the mail from the Hillsborough County Road Department for $6.00. And in addition, "administration charges" in the amount of $2.50!

The practice is called Open Road Tolling (ORT).

Here's how it works: A picture is taken of your car's license plate as it goes through the demolished tollgate area. Your plate number is checked for the owner's address and a bill is sent. *I'm curious about the percentage of payments and what the penalty will be for non-payment. I picture those backward spikes in the road.*

Last Saturday, we went to Miami. That day, most of Miami-Dade County toll roads switched over to ORT. More empty tollbooths. No more pleasant faces. No one to answer questions or give directions. This time the signs read, "DO NOT STOP – CASH NOT ACCEPTED." *By now, I know this is not a gift.*

ORT is occurring throughout the country and friendly employees are dropping by the wayside.

The public library system is encouraging me to use a self-check-out machine for my books. I like my librarian. I like the contact I have with her. We talk about new books and how her children are doing. I told her I did not use the self-check-out because I felt I was putting her out of a job. She assured me librarians had many other things to do than just check out books. Instead of hiring part-time help, a machine is installed. *I don't like it. Another personal contact gone.*

The self-check-out system is insidious. There is one in my grocery store and another in IKEA, a huge box store. You scan your items, insert your credit card, bag your purchases and you're off to your car. No waiting and it looks like fun. And another personal contact gone.

Remember Watson, the computer? IBM challenged *Jeopardy* and its two biggest winners to a game. Watson won.

Watson does not understand nuances. Programmers are now "training" him to assist medical doctors in diagnosing patients. They are not certain how to program patients' body language and word usage for Watson. How will the computer understand these complexities? *This is more than annoying; it is scary. We need to maintain personal contact with our doctors.*

I know I am not ready for any of this.

Are you?

Are you there?

THE PHARMACEUTICAL RIP-OFF

Each day, I take 31 pills, drink a powder dissolved in water and rub something medicinal on my skin. These meds are not designed to heal my ailments. They are created to numb the pain, to ease the symptoms.

I wondered about other people in the same circumstances. They too may feel better, yet be no healthier. Why don't drug companies spend money on research to *cure* illnesses? Because if people are cured, those companies lose their customer base.

Marketing enters the picture, but at what cost? In one year the drug industry spent $31.5 billion on research. What did they spend on advertising? Almost twice as much – $57.7 billion.

Television and print ads present beautiful people and families cavorting in fields of spring flowers. Their vision is clearer; they can walk their dogs and play with their grandchildren. But these people are not cured. Some of their symptoms have been eased.

I hear that quiet, serene voice under the commercial's music – "Side effects may include heart attack, stroke or death." Some of my meds have been recalled. Did people die? How am I? Am I okay? Really?

We are the end consumer, but not the only marketing audience. Students are targeted in medical school. A pre-med student at a prestigious school grew wary as the professor promoted the benefits of a certain medication and belittled a student who asked about side effects. Turns out the professor was not only a full-time member of the medical faculty, but a paid "consultant" to the drug manufacturer.

Troops of sales reps march into doctors' offices. They are attractive, smart and dressed in expense-account clothing. They have almost $10,000 per doctor to be used for whatever will do the trick. Doctors are invited to drug conventions – actually glorious vacations in exotic lands – sponsored by the drug companies.

As part of health care legislation passed in 2010, the government is slated to require drug companies to disclose the money they pay doctors for research, consulting, speaking, travel and entertainment. This sounds like a step in the right direction – if it happens. The regulations are already overdue, and political events could overturn such a law entirely.

"Me-too" drugs, introduced as new treatments, are slight variations of old drugs already on the market. The idea is to grab a lucrative piece of an established market by producing something very similar to a top-selling drug. We now have six statins on the market to lower cholesterol. All are variants of the original.

People are taking a lot more drugs than they used to. Those drugs are likely to be the expensive new ones instead of the older, perfectly good, cheaper kind. Small sample bottles of the newest medications are given to the doctors. They, in turn, ration them out to patients. "Good ole Doctor Jim – he's always got samples. That sure helps the pocketbook."

Once those samples run out, the doctors then prescribe the medication, which is priced at the top of the pyramid. Many patients must choose between drugs and food, with drugs usually losing. Alternatively, people share with a spouse, taking their medicine less often than prescribed.

Listen again to the pharmaceutical ads. Words like *research, innovation, American* are the magic words in public relations messages. These words have little to do with the real picture.

- *Research* is a small part of the big budgets, dwarfed by vast expenditures on marketing and administration.
- The drug industry is not *innovative*. Only a handful of truly new, important drugs have been developed in recent years.
- And the drug companies are far from *American*. More than half of the major firms are headquartered in other countries.

Federal funding for drug research laboratories is falling by the wayside. Pharmaceutical companies are eagerly waiting to pick up the pieces.

Here we are, between a rock and a hard place: The government or corporate entities doing the research, marketing, distribution of our medicines. Does it make a difference who does it?

I don't know. I'm taking two aspirin. I'll get back to you in the morning.

Changing Tides

The tides are constant.
We have no control.

1-800-
We Who Sit and Wait
A Mother's Heart
The Living Will

1-800-

I didn't grieve when Carey died. My friend said, "You've *been* grieving for more than ten years."

Carey was my middle child. She finally succumbed to cancer after a ten-year battle. And what a fight it was. Carey did not go softly into the night. She never went softly anywhere.

For ten years, Carey was in and out of hospitals. It was difficult for her to reach me. Patients could make only collect calls. By the time she got through talking with three or four operators, she was exhausted. I had a toll-free number installed at home. She could call me any time.

Her sense of adventure is legendary and well recognized by our family. I am searching for a photo I call the Demi Moore shot. Carey is mining in the California mountains, very pregnant and very naked except for husky mountain boots.

Carey lived in Daly City, a suburb of San Francisco. The high cliff in the back yard overlooks the Golden Gate Bridge. The zigzag crevasse is the San Andreas Fault Line.

Carey picketed, carried signs and marched for every underdog that needed a champion. She raised three sons and a zoo of small animals. She was a loving, fun mother. She looked after Roger, an injured neighbor, who eventually moved into her home and became family. She baked and cooked with imagination and a light hand. She lived her life with courage and flair and inner strength until her last breath.

Several months before Carey died, we had a family reunion in Key West. Gary, my son, located a waterfront condominium large enough for all of us.

But first, lest you think me a rhymeaphobic, let me explain my children's names.

Jewish custom requires that babies be named for dead relatives. Gary Zach came first and is named for two great-grandfathers. He is known as Gary. No problem.

Then Carey was born and she was named for two grandmothers. Carey Ellen was to be known by both names. That was fine until she got to school. Others in her class would chant "Carry Ellen up the stairs," "Carry Ellen to the cafeteria." She didn't like that, so I told her she could pick a new name. She opted for Itchybottom. That did not last very long. We agreed on Carey.

Sari Lee was named after a grandfather and a grandmother. All was fine until Sara Lee brought her pastries to the public. When Sari Lee finally got to school, her classmates wanted a taste, a bite, anything sweet, preferably with icing. Sari Lee became Sari.

So here I am with Gary, Carey, and Sari. People constantly ask why.

Back to the reunion. Here's who was there:

Gary, his sons, Mike and Drew, and their mother, Chris.

Carey and her youngest son, Andre.

Sari and Rick (her husband).

And me, the Mom.

The adults luxuriated in the splendor of our condominium. The children dove into the bathroom Jacuzzi and played with the jets and bubbles for a while. They got bored and headed for the outdoor pool. The youngest child was still in the Jacuzzi where he promptly pooped. Carey thought it was funny, Gary gagged with laughter breaking through, and Sari cleaned. My three children!

It was Carey who led our parades up and down Duval Street. It was Carey who awakened us at three in the morning. Standing there with her cane, thin as a wraith, shoulders bent, she urged us to go with her and have some fun. We all burrowed deeper into our beds. Carey went out to live.

A few months later, I got the call. Carey had died.

It is a Jewish custom that a 24-hour memorial candle be lit each year on each anniversary of death. I choose to light a candle on her birthday to celebrate her life. Each year the candles have burned 36, 40, 49 hours. It is Carey, who will never allow her light to dim and darken.

I knew her sons would be all right. Jon was an adult and Andre's dad would make a great father for both Andre and Arley. Remember the injured neighbor, Roger, who had moved in? He's still there. Both men would be fine role models for my grandsons.

Thirteen years passed. I had not been in touch with my grandchildren. I lived with the desolation of not knowing the boys – and the guilt of not calling them. I never disconnected the toll free line although it had not rung in thirteen years.

Why? My wise friend said I still could not absorb the reality of Carey's death. By ignoring the boys and keeping the phone, I still felt Carey would call one day.

Go ahead, explain that.

I'm listed in the phone book as M. Gordon. Several months ago I got a call.

"Hello. Is this Marsha Gordon?"

"Yes, it is."

"I'm trying to find my grandmother. This is Andre."

I started to cry.

"We want to be a family, Grandma."

Oh my God.

I called Sari and Gary immediately and, with Rick, we planned to fly to San Francisco. Rick copied old photographs of Carey as a child and teenager. Sari and I made an album for the boys. Jon was now a "mountain man" and there was no way to contact him. He comes down from the mountain infrequently and had recently made his trek to Daly City. There was little chance of seeing him.

Arley, 31, has a responsible job that keeps his family comfortable. I met *my great grandchildren.* Kimi and Kian are beautiful and loving children. Kian is a happy, inquisitive little boy. Kimi is creative and sensitive to other people's feelings. Arley's smile is reminiscent of Carey's. He has Carey's sense of family. His head is completely shaven – a look I like.

Andre, 23, dreams of becoming a San Francisco police officer. He is huge: 230 pounds, 6'4" tall. He's a giant cuddly bear of a man just like his dad. His heart is as big as he is – his mother's heart. He kept looking around the room, proud of his family, proud of what he had accomplished. I told him it was a brave thing he had done, calling after all these years. He said he remembered me as being nice.

Arley and Andre have chosen tender, caring women. There was not a moment of hesitation before we were all tangled in a web of arms and kisses, dampened by joyous tears. I am so proud of them!

We were in San Francisco in November 2009.
It is now April 2010.
Why haven't I called them?
Why haven't I written or emailed?
You can still reach me at 1-800-

WE WHO SIT AND WAIT

Parents sit and wait for children to walk without falling. We wait through elementary school and hope they will escape the bullies. We sit and wait through junior high where the first crush happens. We hope they will not be hurt. We wait through high school where real dating begins, going out at night without adult supervision. That's the tough one. We sit and wait.

Our fourteen-year-old daughter finally convinced us to let her go to one of those night rock concerts teens attended in the seventies. Still do, I guess. She went with her best girlfriend and a group of good friends. We drove them to the concert in Miami and another set of parents was to pick them up.

We sat at home and waited. She was to be home at 12:30, allowing enough time for all the encores.

It was now 1:00. Our daughter was not home. We should have picked her up. Why did we leave it to someone else?

At 1:30, we started calling others in the group to see if they were back. They were.

We called our daughter's best friend. She was home. It was 2:15. She told us, "We got mixed up. We couldn't find the car. But that was okay. A nice man said he'd take us home. He had the cutest dog in the car. He dropped me off about an hour ago."

She lived two blocks from us. We called her back and said we'd pick her up. We wanted her to tell the police all she could about the man, his car and his dog.

It was now 2:45. Time to call the police. An officer was at the house within ten minutes. He took down all the information and told us to stay home and to keep our daughter's friend with us. The police might have more questions for her.

It was a long night. No one spoke. We prayed and we cried together and alone. We paced. We sat and waited.

Fifteen hours later, the police called. They had our daughter. She was okay. Scared and battered but okay. She was at Jackson Memorial Hospital in Miami. We were in Hollywood. It would be a long twenty-minute ride.

There was our daughter waiting for us. She was scratched and bruised, her dress was torn, and her hair was full of grass spurs. She had spent the night in the Everglades in a car with no door handles on the inside. The man had tortured and raped her for thirteen hours. Finally, he dozed off. A window was open about an inch. She quieted the dog and started working on the window, inching it down a small bit at a time. At last, she was able to wriggle out the small open space she had created.

She ran through the Everglades river of sawgrass. The sharp blades cut her face and legs and arms. Her dress was tattered by the stalks. She ran to a construction trailer, the workers just starting for the day. She collapsed on the steps.

The work crew called the police and they took her to Jackson Memorial Hospital's new Rape Crisis Center.

She was safe and in my arms again. We were both trembling.

We need not sit and wait anymore this day.

Robert Carr was captured in the Everglades.

Carr was a serial rapist-murderer who raped or killed at least nine children, boys and girls, from nine to their teens. These children were found between Florida and New England. Who knows? There may have been more victims. We know now of two adult female fatalities.

Robert Carr died in prison in 2007.

A MOTHER'S HEART

I was married at eighteen and a mother at nineteen. People were counting and, to their disappointment, there were eleven months between the wedding and the birth of our son, Gary.

I had no idea how much love could be in a person. I thought I had used it up between friends and family. But there was plenty for Gary.

Two years later, Carey Ellen came along and seven years after that, Sari surprised us all. There was, and is, an abundance of love for each of them.

I know now that the heart expands to house all the love a person has.

Love grows with each smile, each tooth, each first step.

Love grows with each broken arm, each case of the measles.

Love grows with each dance concert and each Little League game.

The Teen Years come too soon: the secret cigarettes and cryptic phone conversations, the clandestine dates and the hidden booze. During those years there were times I didn't like my children. But my love was always there. Never diminished. Never tarnished.

Soon, a daughter-in-law and two sons-in-law came along. There is love for them.

Carey married when she was sixteen and they went off to California. She had a decent life and bore three sons before she became a cancer victim. Carey died after ten years of suffering. My love for her still fills my heart.

There are now five grandsons, and my heart swells with love for this second generation.

And now there is a third generation. The great-grandchildren are here. The fourth one has recently entered my heart.

And still there is enough love for all!

I am off to San Francisco to meet little Nicolas.

THE LIVING WILL

Writing your living will can do you in.

I already have one, created from a template I found on the internet, but something told me it would not suffice. It has been witnessed; my doctors have copies in their files. In fact, one of my doctors has agreed to be the one to give the order. Another doctor, when he heard he was not included, asked to be. I've been called a non-conformist patient before, but *two* doctors willing to pull the plug?

This is the week I've decided to examine this whole thing. I've found my children reluctant to follow my wishes and one doctor has asked to see the new will. He's not sure he wants to be involved anymore. So Sari and I went to an attorney.

What I want is simple and straightforward:

- If my brain is dead, no question – no waiting for anything, just do it.
- If I'm in a resistive vegetative state, go for it.
- If I'm in a coma, wait seven days and pull the plug.
- If I'm an Alzheimer's patient and I don't recognize my children and/or grandchildren and am not interested in their lives, ta-ta. (I've deleted "not remembering names." I can't remember them now.)

- If I'm being kept alive by machines, unplug them.

All reasonable and easily understood, from my point of view.

This document was not acceptable to my children. I told them it was none of their business. It said what I wanted it to say. What a furor this caused.

As a family, we believe in meetings. I asked to schedule a meeting with Sari and Rick. We have brunch every Sunday afternoon. They suggested we discuss it then. "No way," I said. "We need to focus, not be distracted by food." So the meeting was scheduled for after brunch. Time to gather my ammunition.

Somewhere, I have a file named "Bye-Bye" containing papers, accounts, copies of wills. But I can't find it. I asked Rick and within a nanosecond I had everything I had ever given him on the subject. This was good since I didn't have the receipts for the pre-paid cremation or for the captain and boat. But Rick had them.

Okay, why do I need a captain and boat? My ashes will be tossed in two places; half in the Caloosahatchee River and the other half in the salt ponds in Key West. Sari's office is on the river and my son is in Key West. I want to be near both of them and I want them to know I'll be around them most of the time. Depends on the tides.

Captain Vikki and I went for a trial run so I could choose where I wanted to be. Bald eagles flew above the salt ponds. Captain Vikki played

Vivaldi on her Bose and dolphins swam to the boat. There are so many native fish, birds and animals, I'll never be lonely and I'll know my children are near. I couldn't bear to be in a box underground for eternity. Besides, there's not enough room on this earth to bury all of us.

We're at the Sunday meeting with Rick's file and paper and pencil and the discussion begins quietly. It doesn't take long for it to become heated.

<u>I'll never kill you. That's murder.</u>

I give you my permission. I'm asking to be released from pain and/or the terror of being unable to think.

<u>But people come out of comas after years.</u>

I don't want to be in a coma for years.

<u>What if you can hear?</u>

"She looks better today. Not so pale." Or "Poor Marsha, she has so much to live for. I wish she knew about her grandchildren!" Know what? Just let me go!

<u>Isn't it God's choice?</u>

I've had some questions about God's choices, starting in the 20th century and now in the 21st. The way things are going I'd rather make my own decision.

And on it went, voices becoming louder and body language more aggressive. In the middle of it all, my son called from Key West. Sari told him what we were doing. He wouldn't pull anything either but wanted to be there with me.

I realized I wasn't getting much help here, so I told them about Hospice. How Hospice wants to assure quality of life and adheres to requests in living wills. Sari and Rick didn't believe that and assigned to me the task of checking on Hospice's policies.

With that, the meeting came to an end. We hugged and remained friends.

Monday morning I called Hospice. There are several Hospice locations in Lee County and all are listed in the phone book. I randomly chose one. They all follow the same rules. When the right person came on the line, I told him my name and asked my questions. I thought he agreed. I sent an email to Sari and told her so.

I got an email back saying she spoke to the same person. What are the odds on that? Anyway, she asked her questions and he asked, "Is Marsha your mother?" He wasn't sure I understood everything, and I'm certain he did not. He said to Sari, "Your mother is a very strong, independent woman." Sari replied, "Yes, and funny, too."

Now we have an appointment with a Hospice social worker.

I hope I die in my sleep.

.

www.ingramcontent.com/pod-product-compliance
Lightning Source LLC
Chambersburg PA
CBHW060918040426
42445CB00011B/683